WEALTH

10 PRINCIPLES OF

THAT

LEGACY WEALTH

LASTS

JAMES D. SHIELDS

ISBN: Paperback edition 979-8-9889523-1-2
ISBN Kindle edition: 979-8-9889523-0-5

DEDICATION

To my children, all who come after, and
everyone who paved the road before,
May you leave a legacy.

Blessed are those who
plant trees
under whose shade
they will never sit.
-Unknown

CONTENTS

Introduction:
What is Legacy Wealth?

A New Horizon

Once, there was a man named Michael who thrived as an entrepreneur and business leader in New York City. He measured success in tangible achievements: a high-profile career, a luxury apartment overlooking the Manhattan skyline, and a social calendar filled with exclusive events. Life was an exhilarating adventure, and Michael was an enthusiastic participant, always seeking the next big win. But then, a pivotal moment arrived that changed his life. Michael became a parent.

Holding baby Sam for the first time, something profound shifted within. The city lights, once symbols of ambition and success, lost their glow. The endless meetings, the race for promotions, the social galas—none of these things compared to the tiny, breathing miracle cradled in Michael's arms.

Suddenly, the value of time became crystal clear. Every minute spent away from Sam felt like a lost treasure. The drive for professional accolades waned, replaced by an insatiable desire to be present, to witness each of Sam's firsts: the first smile, the first step, the first word.

Michael's priorities shifted dramatically. Wealth was no longer a measuring stick of his value to the world. Instead, money became a tool to create a nurturing environment for Sam, to ensure a secure and educated future. The lavish apartment gave way to a cozy home with a backyard, where Sam could play, discover, and grow up happy.

As Sam grew, so did Michael's perspective on legacy. His legacy was no longer just about financial wealth or a successful career; it was about the values he modeled for Sam. It was about teaching kindness, resilience, and the importance of giving back to the community. For Michael, legacy wealth now meant seeing the world through Sam's curious eyes, shaping a future leader, a compassionate human, someone who would one day make his own mark on the world, grounded in the values passed down from parent to child.

This story is fiction, but it shows the transformative power of parenthood. Children redefine your definitions of success and legacy. As you embark on the journey through "Make Wealth Last: 10 Principles of Legacy Wealth," keep this story in mind. It's a reminder that the greatest legacy you can leave is not the money you have made, but your values, principles, and attitudes that act as seeds planted for future generations. Your legacy is so much more than the accumulation of wealth.

WHAT IS WEALTH?

The word *wealth* comes from the Old English word *wele*, which means well-being. And well-being is about all aspects of your life—mental, physical, emotional, financial, relational and spiritual. Wealth was a much broader concept in earlier times than it is today.

Have you noticed that people who view wealth as only money tend to lose it? I see this repeatedly in my experience as a lawyer and advisor to wealthy families and successful entrepreneurs. The people who chase money don't get wealthy, but those who pursue wealth as well-being are happier, more peaceful, and aligned with their inner purpose. Said another way: *money is part of wealth, but wealth is more than money.*

LEGACY WEALTH IS CREATED

I use the phrase "Legacy Wealth" throughout this book. You may already have glimpsed its meaning, but to be clear, your definition is the most important. Just like

Michael in the story shared at the beginning, it's up to you to decide what values, principles, and attitudes you share with your family as a lasting legacy.

Legacy Wealth is your own internal system of what makes life meaningful and precious.

Legacy Wealth rests on a common set of values. Generational wealth transfer refers to transferring money, yes, but it's more than that: shared values are critical. Without them, it isn't a transfer of Legacy Wealth. Without Legacy Wealth, our children may inherit money, but they will not truly be wealthy.

Wealth, the true, Legacy Wealth that we want to pass on to our children, involves teaching them how to achieve well-being in all areas of life. Legacy Wealth begins with you, and the example you set for your family to achieve it. How do you do this? And what should you include in the legacy—the set of values—you pass on to your children?

Money is inherited, wealth is created.

When you step back from the hectic pace of your life and take the longer view of what you deem vital to your legacy, that is the start of creating Legacy Wealth. The stories and examples I share are what I experienced on my wealth journey. My desire is for you to discover your own wealth values and begin consciously sharing what it means with your family.

THE TREE OF WEALTH

Consider the tree as the symbol of wealth. It started as a seed or acorn and grew into a magnificent specimen because it had fertile soil, rain, and sunlight. The roots spread deep into the earth before the tree gained height above the ground. The roots are the Legacy Wealth Principles and their consistent application produces the mighty tree.

But what if your children only water the leaves and not the roots? Will the tree (your legacy) continue to grow and thrive? Or will the tree eventually lose its footing because the roots were not cultivated and nurtured?

These questions are the ones that keep me up at night. I know you worry about the same things. That is why I wrote this book-to help others cultivate the roots of the tree of wealth by practicing the Legacy Wealth Principles in their family.

WHO AM I?

But, wait. Who, exactly, am I to share this philosophy? Why should you read this book?

As I approach retirement, I think about what will happen to my children when I'm gone. My work has accumulated enough to keep them comfortable for a lifetime, but is comfort what I really want for them? Or is it a value-based, productive life? Would I rather they spend their days climbing, reaching, and overcoming the challenges facing them—or just give them a simple life? As a father, I want my children to be comfortable and have everything they need. And yet, I know that comfort can make people soft and vulnerable, open to the overwhelming obstacles in life.

I wrote this book to share guideposts for my children and grandchildren. My desire is for them to live their lives in meaningful, productive, and creative ways. I also wrote this book for those families who are concerned about more than transferring wealth, who realize that transferring financial means is only part of the equation. Legacy Wealth is about sharing the principles and values that are the foundation (and roots) of a well-lived life.

I have been the principal of The Shields Legal Group for 31 years and CEO of its sister company, The Shields Group for five years. The nature of our practice puts me in a unique situation to work with the wealthy class. As I have advised the wealthy, I have had the opportunity to observe and learn about their relationship to their wealth.

Over the years, I have had interesting conversations with the wealthy, and I always asked them about their greatest concern in life. Many of these people (mostly men) responded in the same way. They expressed their answers differently, but there was a common theme.

Every person was most concerned about their children becoming well-adjusted, productive, and happy members of society. As one wealthy gentleman put it, he didn't want his children "growing up to be derelicts."

This book is the culmination of the wisdom and insights I have gained from these successful people. The "10 Principles of Legacy Wealth" include my decades long observations of wealthy families – what works and what doesn't. This book also includes my own experiences as I have adopted and lived these principles.

I noticed that as I incorporated these intangible concepts of wealth, my life has become wealthy in ways I could never have imagined. Yes, my financial affairs have prospered, but more than that, I see the success of Legacy Wealth in my children as they embrace their lives. I sincerely hope that you recognize yourself in the 10 Principles and commit to sharing them with your loved ones. Create your own version of Legacy Wealth and enrich your family to lead meaningful, purposeful lives.

Chapter 1

CHANGE YOUR ATTITUDE, CHANGE YOUR LIFE

"The last of the human freedoms
is to choose one's attitudes."
—Viktor Frankl

Principle: You can't control your circumstances, but you can control your attitude. Owning this makes everything around us better. A small shift in how you look at the world will lead to a massive change in how you experience it. When you change your attitude, you change your life.

One of my favorite phrases (that I use often) is "Life is good." And I mean it. Life is a joy meant to be experienced every day. Even the midst of difficult situations, life is good.

One day at lunch, I was reminded of the impact of these three simple words. My friend asked how I was doing. He knew that I was handling a difficult client merger, and his tone of voice expressed his concern. I responded with a smile on my face, looked him in the eye and shared, "Life is good!" He laughed and shook his head, saying, "Jim, you never have a bad day." With the right attitude, life *really can* be good.

Even the smallest choices you make affect the rest of your day. Your attitude and perspective have a ripple effect on everyone you encounter. Your very first choice starts when you wake up. Are your thoughts future focused on your to-do list or do you relish the feeing of a warm bed, a secure and safe place to rest?

Begin your day with an attitude of abundance—abundant gratitude, abundant time, and abundant resources. As you tell yourself, "I am so grateful that I slept well last night. I have plenty of time this morning to get ready. I am so grateful for time to linger over coffee with my partner." An abundance attitude opens your awareness of what is possible. It allows you to give of yourself and your time freely and without resentment.

Your attitude affects the start of your day when your spouse, the morning person, flies into the kitchen like a bluebird spotting a worm on the first day of spring. You, (not a morning person), can choose to make this a positive interaction through your attitude.

"Good morning," you say and mean it. You listen and nod along as your spouse describes the "strangest dream" they had last night.

What a pleasant voice they have, you think as you slide into the chair at the far side of the kitchen table, nursing your coffee.

Thirty minutes later, you're five minutes late leaving for work. As you toss the day's belongings into the passenger seat and start the car, you notice the tank is on empty. Your seventeen-year-old borrowed the car out last night and didn't bother to fill it up.

Here it is: another choice.

Ah, what's done is done, you think, and back out of the driveway. You'll fill up at Buc-ees, the mega-gas station on your way. Not ideal when you're running late for work, but not the worst scenario either. *I can grab another cup of coffee while I'm there*, you think, putting a positive spin on this morning's events once again.

When it's your turn to pay for your coffee, the attendant looks at you with an expression of vague disinterest.

"That'll be three dollars fifty-six," she says, smacking her gum between the words.

"How are you today?"

Her face lights up briefly. "It's been crazy! I worked the night shift and now I'm on overtime because Jeremy didn't come in. They won't hire anyone else, and they'll fire me if I go home." She sighed deeply with resignation. "So here I am."

You smile at her again and hold her gaze, letting her know you see her as a person. As you pick up your coffee, you slide a ten-dollar bill across the counter. "Please use this to buy something for yourself." Gratitude fills her eyes as she whispers, "Thank you!"

Positivity breeds positivity. You can choose to dwell on negative instances and perceive them as personal attacks on your good humor, or you can look for ways to add value and improve the situation.

THE ATTITUDE PIVOT CHECKLIST

Your attitude is often the only thing you can control. As you move through your day and you notice that your attitude has turned negative or limited, step back and ask yourself if you can see the situation differently. For example,

- When a coworker makes a mistake, do you dwell on the mistake or focus on the opportunity to be a mentor and help?

- Do you look for ways to add value at work, or simply do your job to earn a paycheck?
- Is your word reliable and dependable?
- Are you honest with people, both in your actions and your silence?
- Are you willing to move in a different direction, even if it means you might make a mistake?

Attitude is the difference between a wealthy person and a poor person. The poor in spirit believe most of life is out of their control and happens to them. The rich in spirit and well-being (and often money) know that their attitude is within their control. Knowing you can choose your attitude changes everything-- your day, your life, and your future legacy.

But what if you are stuck in a negative attitude that has become a habit? One you no longer think about because it is so ingrained. You have a choice in that situation too.

CHANGE YOUR ATTITUDE TO CHANGE YOUR HABITS

If you want to change your life, begin by identifying the attitude that created your habits. According to James Clear, author of "Atomic Habits,"

We want solutions, but what we
really need are attitudes.
Attitude precedes outcome." - *James Clear*

When you choose a poor attitude—and it really is a choice, even when it doesn't feel like it—your actions are different than when you are in a positive frame of mind. Maybe you're having a bad day or your internal chemistry is off and it's easier to be sullen than joyful. Whatever the reason, you have now set a precedent. The next time this same trigger occurs, it'll be easier to turn negative in your reactions to people and act in a way that is unhelpful and uncaring.

Small choices made over and over soon become a habit. You slip into repeating this behavior, not because it is right or because it is in your best interest, but because you are not conscious of it. It just feels... normal. And once you've adopted the negative attitude a few times, the pattern takes root and become stronger and stronger. Over time, your ability to choose a different attitude is masked by the habitual behavior.

Websters defines "habit" as "an acquired mode of behavior that has become nearly or completely involuntary." When you allow negative or judgmental attitudes to become a habit, your perspective changes and the decisions you make directly impact the outcome.

The opposite can also be true. When I remind myself that "today is a good day," I notice that I see more of what is good. Small or inconvenient disturbances do not impact my peace of mind, because it's included in today being a good day.

The difference in outcomes of a positive or negative attitude is obvious when you begin to pay attention. And that's the point – to unravel your habitual behavior and identify the foundational attitude that allowed the habit to develop.

John was an older gentleman who became my mentor. He used to remind me that, "You can see yourself as a victim or as a victor. The choice is always yours." Whenever I notice that I am blaming someone or something, I think of him. And then I step back and look at the situation from a victor's attitude. The change in attitude and perspective opens my eyes to the possibilities that were always there, but I couldn't see them.

Be careful not to see yourself as a "victor" over other people. When John shared the distinction between a victim and a victor attitude, he made sure I understood what he meant by "victor." It didn't mean I was better than or superior; instead, being a "victor" meant that I had overcome my own tendency to choose a negative, judgmental or limiting attitude.

When you focus on how you've been wronged in life, you naturally develop a negative attitude towards life. Your ability to control external events is hampered by the "victim" mentality that things happen to you. In contrast, the "victor" attitude sees the situation from an optimistic view and acknowledges that the events may not have happened as expected. You can still influence the outcome with a positive attitude and gratefulness for the good in the situation.

LEGACY WEALTH IS FUELED BY YOUR ATTITUDE

Wealth is so much more than your bank balance. Attitude, which is always under your control, is where Legacy Wealth is born. When your attitude is negative and remains unchecked, you may start down a destructive path. Suppose, for example, that you were aggressive at work and got disciplined. On the way home, you expressed your rage on the road and caused an accident that hurt other people. Because you didn't manage your anger, your actions had severe consequences.

Choose an attitude of positivity, optimism, constantly searching for opportunities.   Living from a positive attitude essentially affects the wealth you enjoy in your life. The more positive you are, the more successful you become, and the more choices you have. When you look for opportunities, you are not afraid of change and your heart overflows with gratitude.

A natural consequence of a wealth attitude is that you will naturally attract others with a similar energy. Negative, judgmental, and victim-minded people tend to fall away from your life, because you no longer support their poor attitude. It comes down to a simple formula:

Wealth attracts opportunities to create more wealth.
Judgment attracts opportunities to judge more.

Wealthy people, those who choose an attitude of abundance and gratitude, simply don't want to be around others who are negative, focus on the bad, constantly grind on the past, and blame others for their circumstances. This is an obvious truth. If you choose to increase your wealth through a change in your attitude, spend time with other wealthy people.

BEGIN – THE REST IS EASY

My father was a lawyer for more than fifty years. Whenever I went to his office as a child, he would let me sit in his swivel chair. I would spin around until I was too dizzy to stand. He always enjoyed seeing me having fun in the same place where he worked and provided a service that supported his family.

One day, after I had spun the chair harder than ever, it took longer for me to stop being dizzy. When my dad could see that I was back to normal, he picked up a sign from his desk and handed it to me. It said: "Begin. The rest is easy."

I must have looked confused, because when I gave the sign back to him, he said something I have never forgotten. He looked me in the eye and said, "Jim, most people think too much about how to begin. You make progress when you overcome the fear of beginning."

I share that story to illustrate that now is the best time to begin changing your attitude. It doesn't matter that you were negative or judgmental yesterday, or you have been carrying the past on your back for decades. Today is the day it all changes.

Based on my experience of living on this earth for more than six decades, I have discovered there are three activities that you can begin today. No training is needed, no special skills are required. Instead, only a commitment to begin.

1. Begin each day with a morning ritual. I use the first hour to meditate, journal, and set my

intentions for the day. Since I began this practice, I have noticed that it sets the tone for my day. I am more resilient and flexible when something goes wrong, and I am able to see the opportunities in every situation to grow, change, or pivot. Make the first hour of every day your opportunity to choose how you react and respond to your world.

2. <u>Remind yourself there are two sides to every coin.</u> Before rushing to judgment, allow yourself time to learn about both sides of the situation. When your attitude remains neutral and you trust those around you, the conflict becomes clear and resolution possible. No one can see all sides of a problem, but when you take the time to identify what can be seen, you will manage the people involved in a kind, compassionate, and Wealth Legacy way.

3. <u>Confide in a person you trust</u> and ask them to help you develop a more positive attitude. Ask that person to hold you accountable and accept their feedback with a desire to see your blind spots. Having a trusted friend or loved one be a sounding board or a mirror is great way to understand how your conduct affects other people.

Changing your attitude by making a new choice takes courage. It takes courage to acknowledge that you want to change, to invest in yourself and your choices, and to accept the consequences of your decisions. Be forewarned—when we change our lives, we always make mistakes. It's a part of the human experience. But the most successful people I know have made many mistakes. The key is to view mistakes as opportunities and part of a positive attitude.

DAILY PRACTICE: REMIND YOURSELF TO BE POSITIVE

Journaling helps me develop a positive mindset and an attitude of self-reflection. I recommend doing this daily. Each morning, get out your journal and begin by writing three positive affirmations for yourself for the day—these are things you know to be true about yourself but sometimes need to be reminded of. It might be something as simple as, "I am a good person" or "Life is happening for me, not to me." In my case, I remind myself that I am a child of God and that all abundance is available to me. Whatever it is, keep it short and memorable. Remember: these are things you know to be true about yourself or want to be true. You can't deceive yourself, but you can encourage yourself with affirmations to shake you out of a negative cycle and focus on the good in your life.

Underneath these affirmations in your journal, state your intention for the day. For example, one of my intentions every morning is to have the humility to own my mistakes. As you reflect on your intention, say your affirmations as a way to program your mind. You might even go into the bathroom and say your affirmations as you look at yourself in the mirror.

Controlling your attitude is a habit that takes practice, but once you have a greater awareness of yourself and your actions, you'll notice that your days feel more peaceful than chaotic, and every problem has a solution—as long as you know where to look.

The natural consequence of choosing a positive attitude consistently is gratitude.

Experiencing gratitude leads to more places to express gratitude. It feeds on itself and reinforces positive events in your life. As you find more openings to pay it forward, others respond in kind. Taking the small step of expressing gratitude to someone daily will soon become habit-forming and life-changing.

Success breeds success. Positivity breeds more of the same. As you consider the intangible gifts you are leaving to future generations, a positive attitude is the beginning. You can see the possibilities and solutions and that leads to the second Legacy Wealth Principle: Gratitude.

Chapter 2

SAY "THANK YOU" FOR EVERYTHING

"Acknowledging the good that you already have in your life is the foundation for all abundance."
—Eckhart Tolle

Principle: The easiest way to be happy is to say "thank you" more often. Not just for the good things in life but also for the "bad." Challenges and frustrations that we may label as "bad" ultimately make us better. Gratitude creates happiness. It possesses the power to shape our situations and create success in every sense of the word. If you want to be happier, say thank you... for everything.

In 2017, I attended a retreat at the Catholic Conference and Formation Center in Dallas, Texas, where author

Chris Lowney spoke about his book, *Heroic Leadership*. One part of his talk really stuck out to me, and I would even dare to say what I gleaned from it is an underrated secret to success - The Power of Gratitude.

The retreat was an opportunity to learn from others about faith-based leadership. I thought we would discuss more traditional leadership strategies and techniques that are mainstream business school like ideas. Instead, we spent time on other traits that should be core leadership ideals, including gratitude. The premise, which I have now adopted, is that effective leadership starts with gratitude. As we acknowledge the people, events, and circumstances that enable us to create meaning in our lives, it opens the door for more of the same to flow through.

We are all leaders in some fashion - we lead by our own actions; whether at work or at home. The ripple effect of this retreat on leading through gratitude is that years later, I still focus on the practice of gratitude that helps create generational and Legacy Wealth.

Gratitude isn't a new concept. In fact, we're so accustomed to hearing about gratitude that its true value has become diluted. Let us take a moment to reexamine the simple, profound power of gratitude and how it can shape our days and our lives.

Gratitude has the power to shape a situation, our

health, and yes, even our finances. When we live in gratitude, our perspective on individual situations and our lives changes. Dr. Robert Emmons, Ph.D., a leading gratitude scientist, has studied the effects of gratitude on behavior. He has come to the conclusion that gratitude is essential to life, especially when life becomes hard. Dr. Emmons distinguishes between the *feeling* of gratitude and *being* grateful. Feelings are transitory and spring from how we look at the world. According to his research, "being grateful is a choice...when disaster strikes, gratitude provides a perspective from which we can view life in its entirety and not be overwhelmed by temporary circumstances."

Being grateful and expressing it gives us a huge health benefit—happiness. Gratitude shows you how to replace negativity with positivity and helps you be actively thankful for your surroundings. When you express gratitude, positive emotions are the result. Staying positive improves your health, prepares you for hard times, and creates stronger relationships. Being gratitude means choosing to see good in a person or situation, even when you may think no good can come of it.

Without gratitude, a chasm is created that allows negativity to flood into your thoughts and your life. If you aren't grateful for what you already have, what you have will never be enough. This prompts a never-ending journey of searching for "more" and seeking control of others, bending them to your will and expectations in order to make you "happy." When you are grateful for what you already have, the constant striving for more ends. Instead of being dissatisfied, you are full of gratitude.

Gratitude Is a Habit, not a Feeling

Expressing gratitude has short-term rewards, but its real power lies in making it a lifetime habit. As you experience being grateful for even the smallest things, you will notice more opportunities to be grateful. Over time, it becomes a habit that is rewarding on many levels.

I began a gratitude-based practice in my office years ago. My team is action-oriented, and because of this, we're problem-solvers. We established a gratitude framework when discussing solutions to conflict and problems in the office. Whenever someone presents a problem, we'll consider a positive solution by focusing on two things. First, we work to clearly understand the issue and second, we have a solution-based mindset. This transforms the discussion from a mere complaint to one accompanied by an action-based solution. Gratitude encourages us to think of solutions, not just problems.

When you think about it, gratitude can be felt at any time, for any reason. Expressing gratitude is like driving down the interstate, looking out the windshield. You check the rearview mirror occasionally to make sure no one's riding your bumper, but the horizon and cars ahead of you hold most your focus. You can experience gratitude by looking forward or behind, but it's the forward-focused gratitude that keeps you moving ahead. It is a choice to be a windshield person, not a rear-view mirror person.

I recently had lunch scheduled with a colleague I wasn't especially close to and hadn't seen for a while. I had many pressing matters to handle that day, and I wasn't looking forward to being away from the office. Instead of resenting the fact that I couldn't get out of the lunch, I decided to go and be grateful for the opportunity. The time together allowed us to connect on a deeper level, and I now consider him to be more than an acquaintance. The lunch was a "windshield opportunity" to look forward to the future. Gratitude does that.

The power of gratitude causes ripples of impact on everyone around you. I have a friend who spent his work life building several technology companies. After he retired, he opened a food bank out of a desire to make a difference and give back. He expressed gratitude for what he had by sharing it with others. He and his wife have distributed millions of meals to children, and their organization continues to grow. I commented to him recently that it must feel good to make such a positive impact on the city. His response? He was grateful for the opportunity to serve the children in our community. Gratitude in action has a widening impact on the larger community.

The expression of gratitude inevitably leads to a solution-focused set of priorities. And these solutions can be with issues at home or work, or within our communities. Every problem has a solution, and gratitude for the opportunity to learn opens our minds to a solution-based mindset. Here's a checklist I use to ensure I express gratitude throughout my day:

- When I wake up, before I do anything else, I say I am thankful to have woken up today.
- As I'm getting dressed, I reflect on who I want to be today and am thankful for the opportunities I'll have throughout the day.
- Whenever I feel irritation or anger, I use this as a reminder to find one thing I'm grateful for in the instigating situation.
- By lunchtime each day, I make sure I've thanked at least one person (but hopefully more!) for something they've done.

WHEN GRATITUDE SHOWS
UP AT YOUR DOOR

I was at home one evening when there was a soft knock on the front door. A young mother was standing outside with her daughter, who was about 9 years old. The mother introduced herself and Jessica as our neighbors. Then she gestured for her daughter to explain why they were knocking on people's doors.

Jessica looked up at me and smiled. "I love to bake, and I am actually good at it."

I smiled at her to continue, silently admiring her innocent ability to acknowledge that she was good at something she enjoyed.

Her expression became earnest as she continued. "I heard about kids my age not having enough to eat when school is out for the summer." She looked down and paused, then continued. "I have all the food I could ever eat. It just didn't seem fair that I don't have to worry about what's for dinner when these kids go to bed with no food."

I was speechless and nodded for her to continue. Jessica held up a tray of cookies that looked delicious. She said, "I decided I would bake everything I could and sell it, so the money could help feed kids."

I looked at her mother in astonishment. She said, "Jessica is having her bake sale tomorrow. Would you please support her?"

For a few seconds, my voice was caught in my throat. I squatted down to be at eye-level with Jessica. "You just taught me a lesson in giving I will never forget." I smiled at her and assured them that we would be happy to support her bake sale. As we said goodbye and I closed the door, I knew I would always remember that moment of connection with a 9-year-old girl who gave from her abundance to help others.

Jessica was giving of her time, talent, and energy from an overwhelming sense of gratitude and abundance. There was no agenda, no need for recognition, no loud voices or trumpets proclaiming her worth. Instead, Jessica knew in her heart that kids shouldn't go hungry, and she wanted to change that sad fact. Gratitude in action is a beautiful sight.

DAILY PRACTICE: KEEP A HABIT JOURNAL

Gratitude, like all habits, requires practice before it becomes second nature. As I mentioned in the previous chapter, I start every morning writing in my journal. No matter how I feel when I wake up, or what will happen the rest of the day, I try to jot down a few things that I am grateful for. This practice focuses my mind on the goodness of life and grounds my morning with a feeling of positivity.

As much as we all may like to plan, the truth is life is unpredictable, and we don't know what the day will throw at us. What we do know is that we can always control our attitude toward unexpected happenings. Setting your emotional tone and attitude on gratitude before your feet hit the floor is a proven way to have a great day. Choosing to be grateful for everything, even the little things, guarantees an uplifting experience.

Your first course of action is to keep a daily gratitude journal. The written word is a powerful medium, and you can use the journal as a point of reference to look back on in the future. It doesn't have to be long, just write a few sentences every day about who and what you are grateful for. Remember: as you expand your awareness of gratitude, you expand your capacity to be grateful.

The second action to practice gratitude regularly is to write a thank-you note to people who are important in your life. Remember the words of Robert Emmons: "Gratitude is an affirmation of goodness." Affirm the goodness of the people in your life and how their goodness has affected you. Gratitude pays itself forward and will create a reciprocal sense of others being grateful to you. This will remind you of who you appreciate in your life and why and make you feel better about yourself and your life. They will return the favor, and you'll feel even better. Gratitude really is the ultimate life hack, as it only makes everything better.

Finally, use words of gratitude throughout your day to express thankfulness for the little things. Imagine you're on your way to work and hit each red traffic light. Now you have a few more minutes of silence in your car before you hit the ground running for the day. Look for the gifts all around you and appreciate them. Use the practice of daily gratitude to improve your life and see how it transforms your mind, relationships, and even your finances. Whether you want them to, things in your life are just going to happen. Some of them will appear to be good and some will not; that's just the way it goes. But when you choose to be grateful for it all, it all becomes a gift. Say "thank you" to everything, and you will always have a reason to be grateful. Gratitude fosters a wealthy mindset, which creates a wealthy life.

As a positive attitude leads to gratitude, possibilities present themselves. Through your work and success, you have discovered your passion and now it's your hope that your children find their passion. Let's turn to Legacy Wealth Principle #3 – Passion.

Chapter 3
Don't Find Your Passion— Develop It

"I have no special talents. I am only passionately curious."
—Albert Einstein

Principle: Prosperity follows passion. We can't change the world if we don't first listen to what lights us up on the inside. When we find the intersection of our skills, passion, and needs of the world, that's where we will prosper. Passion is not found; it's created.

After graduating from law school, I started my journey to define my purpose by making as much money as possible. I wanted to prove myself to my parents under the now-mistaken belief that if I made more money and bought more material possessions, the world would recognize me as a success. I got caught up in a materialistic society and placed value on accumulation of money and things. This is a common approach many young people take, and it's not wrong, per se; but only leads to wanting more.

In my case, I focused on possessions, not people. One day, my beautiful and ever-patient wife explained to me the error in my thinking. She helped me realize money was not a goal, a destination, or anything to strive for. Money was simply a tool, a means to reach a more fulfilling life. And over time, we changed our buying habits from accumulating possessions to creating experiences. We took our kids on some amazing outdoor vacations, skied together, traveled in an RV to beautiful destinations, and spent a lot of time on the soccer and baseball field.

A new car, a new house, or spending time with a new toy is always fun. After a while, though, when the excitement wears off, you may wonder why you were excited. As the original Spock says, "After a time, you may find that having is not so pleasing a thing after all as wanting. It is not logical, but it is often true." He means that the pursuit is more important than the thing pursued. I can say the same of passion.

Many people today talk about finding their "passion," but this is a misnomer. You don't find your passions, like some mysterious treasure you stumbled across accidentally. Everyone has passions. The challenge and the opportunity occur when you decide, intentionally, to pursue your passion. This pursuit gives meaning to your efforts. Passion rarely works like a lightbulb that gets turned on in a single moment. More often, you have to diligently and purposefully pursue your passion. As Angela Duckworth says: "A passion is developed more than it is discovered." It takes time and even tenacity to reveal the spark that makes your life shine.

Do we need passion to live a rich life? Some might say no, that all you need is to focus on a few key strategic areas, and you will succeed. But I disagree. You can't really live without passion. You can *endure* a life that way, but you can't *live* one. Passion:

- Gives you the drive to pursue a goal with vigor and perseverance;
- Points you in the direction that will ultimately lead to success; and
- It is the fuel for the fire of your life.

Once you've pursued your passion and wrestled it to the ground (because sometimes that's what it takes), identify why you are passionate, and *voilá*. You've written a recipe for joy-filled success.

Why Does a Bird Sing?

I once heard a story about a college professor who was widely acclaimed to be the leading expert in his area. His passion for the subject was displayed every time he taught in front of his class, and the students loved him for it. His popularity grew to where the college had to move his classes into the largest auditorium on campus.

One day, a newspaper reporter came to campus to interview the professor and discover the secret to his popularity. The reporter asked him, "What difference do you hope to make in the world?"

The professor was silent for several seconds, then replied, "I have no such hopes. I know that the students who are ready to hear what I have to share will take it in. Those who aren't ready or willing, won't."

The reporter was shocked. "Why do you keep teaching?"

The professor smiled at the younger man, waited a beat, and then said, "Why does a bird sing?"

Your passion is how you find meaning in your life. It's the North Star of your inner world and what you're to share. When you allow your passion to be expressed fully, the whole world notices and sings with you.

IDENTIFYING YOUR PASSION

Passion isn't a single-moment discovery. It's rarely a "eureka" experience and more often a "Where do my energies best fit right now?" question to be answered over a long period. Move in a direction that interests you, while being open to what you discover about yourself along the way. Again, this is something that is developed, and over time, you gain greater confidence in what you might eventually come to think of as a calling or vocation.

I use the Venn Diagram strategy in Figure 1 below when guiding people to their passions.

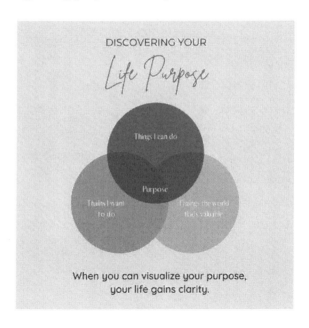

DISCOVERING YOUR

Life Purpose

Things I can do

Purpose

Things I want to do

Things the world finds valuable

When you can visualize your purpose, your life gains clarity.

In one circle, I write "Things I can do." In the second circle, I write "Things I want to do." In the third circle, I write, "Things the world finds valuable." All three circles overlap in the center. Your passion lies in that center space.

I paid my way through law school by working on a construction crew building houses. I strutted around all day with a tool kit strapped around my waist and a hammer in my right hand. That summer, my hammer was basically an added appendage. I became very familiar with the 2x4's used to build single and multi-family housing. I was good at it.

If I were to use the Venn Diagram to find my passion during law school, I would write "Use a hammer" on my "Things I can do" list. I could also build cabinets, pour concrete, and read a set of construction plans. Even though I has these skills, I knew I didn't want to work in construction. Creating a list for the first circle requires honesty, and it's a great exercise to develop a list of your skills. Don't focus on what you want to do, but simply on what you know how to do.

The Second Circle contains a list of things that you want to do. Contrary to the First Circle, this second list includes both items that you are currently good at that fuel your passion, and stretch goals, those things that you have tried and may not be good at, but enjoy and want to improve upon. Completing the Second Circle provides an opportunity to explore the breadth and reach of your aspirations and goals. Regardless of your skill level and experience with any items on the second list, there's always room for improvement. Focusing on enjoyable activities and fueling your desire to improve involves stoking your passion for the task at hand.

The Third Circle includes the activities that the world around you perceive as valuable. To be effective in evaluating the Third Circle, include activities and skills that are valuable now and will also be valuable in the future. Seek advice from mentors, friends, business associates, and people you trust to evaluate future trends and opportunities.

Note that the Third Circle isn't "what the world will pay for." It's what the world needs. Your passion may be the creation of a new cellular phone (Steve Jobs), developing a new software platform (Bill Gates), or focusing on converting the world to sustainable energy and electric vehicles (Elon Musk). These men followed their passion, and they were successfully rewarded. But that's not the test. There are equally passionate people who devote their passion to charitable causes, setting up remote water treatment facilities, and feeding the poor. These people are just as wealthy as Bill Gates, just not as rich.

Focus on what the *world* needs now and, in the future, instead of what *you* can provide to the world. I suspect that the last buggy whip manufacturer, who rode the demand for their product to the bottom as cars were being mass produced, thought he was producing the very best product on the market. Soon the world changed, and cars replaced horses, so the buggy whip was no longer needed. Successful companies working in an obsolete industry survive by understanding what the market needs and adapting to those changing needs. In evaluating what the world views as valuable, look at the demand and consumer needs, not your skills. If you focus inward, only on your skills, your ability to experience passion through your actions could face a serious challenge brought on by change. You could soon become a contemporary buggy whip maker.

This simple exercise hinges on one fundamental premise: that you take action and do *something*. For change to happen, it requires effort. As Brian Tracy, a world-renowned motivational speaker and author notes, "A wish has been defined as a goal with no energy behind it. Hope is not a strategy."

Actions require deliberate, conscious, and focused attention. Pursue your passion intentionally and one step at a time. We all do our best work and find our greatest joy at the intersection of the things we can do, the things we want to do, and what the world values.

This sounds like a simple exercise, but you have to be honest with yourself when you examine these three things. Here's a <u>Passion Identification Checklist</u> to get you started:

- What motivates you?
- Think of a recent situation that you responded to with joy. What triggered that response?
- Now think of a recent situation where you felt sad, angry, or hurt. Again, what caused that response?
- Do you respect the opinions of others?
- Do you take direct and indirect cues when your actions or behavior affect someone around you? How do you respond?

DAILY PRACTICE: THE "WHY" EXERCISE

Honesty will, in the long term, always prevail. It will help you build the right relationships, cultivate peace in your life, and build trust with friends and colleagues. Be honest, even in the little things and with yourself. Being honest is the first step in finding the purpose behind your passion. Give yourself an honest look in the mirror and ask an important and oft-overlooked question: "Why?"

I adapted the following exercise from the work of Simon Sinek (check out his most well-known work, *Start with Why* if you want to go deeper in this). Take out your journal and write this question at the top of the page, filling in the blank with your goal:

Why do I want to _____?

When you've written the answer to that question, ask yourself again: *Why?* And when you have the answer to that question, ask yourself again. And again. And again. And again. Once you've asked *why* five times, then you have your real, genuine answer. Digging deep helps you understand your passions, and when you understand why they exist, you know how to use them.

As mentioned at the beginning of this chapter, when pursuing money for the sake of itself, I realized I could make good decisions in my business and personal life, but my "why" was based on materialistic goals—and in the end, these choices weren't very fulfilling. The things I acquired actually weren't what I wanted; they represented what I thought I wanted. Upon examination, I realized what I really wanted were deeper and more meaningful experiences. If I had never asked *why* repeatedly, I never would have known this and would have continued to feel frustrated at why getting the things I thought I wanted wasn't making me happy. The reason behind our decisions is just as important as the decisions themselves.

Part of my purpose, business and personal, is to focus on improving the lives of people. Shields Legal is a people-centric organization instead of product or service-centric. Our business philosophy rests on the concept that if we invest in people and align our purpose, there won't be a bad outcome. Unexpected things still happen, but it's much easier to course correct when you understand the underlying purpose.

Your passion and purpose aren't just found; you create it through careful reflection and diligent pursuit. You don't merely discover your passion; you develop it. Your children will notice when you are passionate about a project, business, or hobby. As you explore your passions, you give your children permission to do the same. The examples you set for your children are part of your family's Legacy Wealth.

Have you ever asked your children if they know the "why" behind your success? Have you shared stories with them about the crossroads you faced and "why" you went left instead of right? Legacy Wealth includes the "why" behind your business or financial status. When you share it with your children and connect to their "why," everyone benefits.

The next Legacy Wealth Principle can be difficult. Taking responsibility is a mature response to the unexpected. Accepting your part in the situation can ease tensions, reduce anxiety and foster the connection with your family.

Chapter 4

QUIT THE BLAME GAME— TAKE RADICAL RESPONSIBILITY

> *"Authenticity is everything! You have to wake up every day and look in the mirror, and you want to be proud of the person who's looking back at you. And you can only do that if you're being honest with yourself and being a person of high character. You have an opportunity every single day to write that story of your life."*
> —Aaron Rodgers

Principle: The mirror never lies. If you want to become better, you have to be honest with yourself—about yourself. Taking radical responsibility for your situation is the best way to control the chaos of life. Lack of success isn't due to lack of opportunity; it's due to lack of awareness. And before you can change anything, you first have to own the fact that regardless of the event, you're involved and therefore have some responsibility for the outcome.

Acknowledging your involvement is the first step to taking control of a situation. Our actions, reactions and perspective require responsibility before we can influence the result.

Several years ago, I had a meeting with five different CEOs of five different companies. They were all in different fields: commercial real estate, logistics, healthcare, automotive, and commercial landlord. The executives of all five companies faced similar problems, but none of the leaders believed they were at fault. Each leader sought solutions to make the "other guy" pay. The problems we discussed involved a senior executive, a critical vendor, and a customer issue.

The gist of my conversations with the CEOs had a common theme: they were all pointing their finger at someone else as the cause of the problem. They only wanted to talk about what the other person did wrong, their inappropriate behavior, and how this person's decisions negatively affected the business. It was consistently someone else's fault, and that theme permeated each situation. Because the lens through which these CEOs were evaluating the issues focused on the other person's decisions, any solutions that they wanted to discuss involved how to control the other person.

When you don't view conflicts as mirror opportunities, you may find yourself blaming someone else for your problems. Responsibility for correction lies with them, not you, right? The direct result of this strategy, as you've probably noticed, is that often you give control to the other person to make decisions that can materially impact you. By putting the blame on someone else for what happens in your life, you give away your power and remain stuck, waiting for them to change. Blaming others also relieves us of self-reflection and self-evaluation, because we use the excuse, "it was their fault" instead of determining how our actions influenced the result. The victim mentality is a losing paradigm, and it's a cycle that, unless corrected, will always repeat itself.

Of the five CEOs I met that day, one of them made a comment that amazed me. He said he wanted to evaluate his and his team's behavior to determine what action caused or complicated the problem. Then he wanted to determine what actions they could take to solve the problem and get the result they need. This solution-based mindset led him to creating a new position in the company responsible for vetting critical vendors and building relationships with them, because he realized that the company was not doing a good job in vendor management. He took radical responsibility of his and his company's mistakes, then set a process in place to prevent the same mistake from being made in the future.

The other four CEOs did two things with their choice to blame someone else for the problem: They ceded control of their company to the person they blamed, and they created an environment primed for self-inflicted wounds. Each of these leaders were intelligent, knowledgeable, and good leaders, but they failed to look at their own actions to see how it impacted the situation.

If I were to share just one pet peeve I have in business, it would be self-inflicted wounds. These are foreseeable problems that could have been expected and avoided with a bit of planning and thought. Can you see how the victim mentality comes full circle? By not self-reflecting in situations of conflict and recognizing what these business leaders could have done differently, they will probably repeat the same mistake in the future, again and again. As the famous saying goes, "The definition of insanity is doing the same thing over and over and expecting different results."

There is another perspective and attitude. It's called "Radical Responsibility" and it is a key principle of Legacy Wealth. When you take responsibility, you regain power.

The only person you can change is yourself. Once that law of human behavior becomes part of your mental and emotional structure, you'll discover you have more authority and power than you may have realized.

AN EXERCISE IN RADICAL RESPONSIBILITY

Besides looking at your own decisions, Radical Responsibility includes the power to choose your perspective. You have choices to make and can control how you interpret and respond to any event. For example, I know you have seen other drivers who make really poor decisions on the road. There is always a choice of how to respond: either you get angry and escalate the situation, or you can take a deep breath and control your behavior. Are we really going to let someone else's poor decisions affect our actions when we have the choice to decide otherwise?

Before pointing the blame at someone else, ask yourself the Radical Responsibility Questions listed below. These questions are designed to refocus your attention on finding a solution to the problem, instead of assigning blame.

Think of a situation where you have blamed someone else, and write down the facts. Facts are objective and verifiable. Do not include your judgments, blame, or criticism. After you have identified the facts of the situation, make a note next to each fact about whether you had any influence or control. Then, ask yourself the Legacy Wealth Radical Responsibility Questions listed below and answer each question as honestly as possible.

- What could I have done differently?
- What actions did I take that may have contributed to this?
- What can I do now to fix the situation?

As you look over the facts, your decisions and actions, and your answers to the Radical Responsibility Questions, what is your conclusion? Do you see your part in the creation of the event? What can you do now to remedy it?

This exercise in Radical Responsibility applies to business, family and relationships. Once you begin to see your role in creating the conflict or problem, you regain your power to choose again. If you've been blaming others for the problems, you had a hand in creating—even if was only because you let happen-try pausing and asking the three Radical Responsibility Questions. Your mind will begin to look for solutions and so will your team and family.

WINNING MEANS LEARNING TO PLAY WELL

One year, my family went to a baseball tournament with my middle son. We hired a coach to prepare for this tournament, and he spent weeks getting the team ready. Even though they practiced long past when the field lights turned off, the team didn't play well in the tournament. However, in true current fashion, all the kids received medals for participating. When my son, Matthew, walked back to the bleachers to show me his medal, I put my hand on his shoulder and said, "Son, I'm proud of how hard you worked, and nothing will change that. But you didn't earn that medal." I looked deeply into his eyes before adding, "Instead, you earned a lesson on how to play better."

Matthew's eyes flashed with anger, then hurt, and he walked back to the dugout with his shoulders drooped so low they could have tagged second base. It was a tough moment for him, but I wanted him to understand that we succeed in baseball, as we do in life, when we set goals, learn, and achieve results. We don't create wealth through mere effort; rather, we create wealth through deliberate actions that lead to results. His team hadn't done that. They failed to achieve the result they wanted—they lost. There's no shame in that, but there's also no celebration. It created a powerful opportunity to learn, grow, and get better.

After the tournament, my son was mad at me for several days, but we got through it. He eventually let go of his resentment. But when his baseball team started winning, he understood that success feeds on and reinforces itself. He realized he had truly earned his new trophies. Participation alone is not enough. Understand the rules, play to win and take responsibility when you lose.

Another story illustrates this point. After the Philadelphia Eagles lost the Super Bowl on February 12, 2023, Jalen Hurts, the Eagles' quarterback, spoke in the press conference. When he was asked how he felt about the loss (38-35), he said something that resonated with me. His answer to the question was, "You know, it's not about winning or losing. It's really about winning or learning."

Do you see the difference? Setting up every situation as a "win or loss" means there are winners and losers. One person is up while the other person is down. This perspective is no way to live your life, and it certainly doesn't help the "loser" triumph. Reframe the situation as either "winning or learning" and watch what happens to your team or your family. Instead of being unworthy or insufficient, learning offers opportunities to become better.

At the heart of regret is failing to recognize that you control how you view what happens to you. This is what

I hoped to teach my son during his baseball tournament, and what I've worked to instill in all my children. When you take Radical Responsibility for your view of life, "win or learn" opens the door to continued success. You are either winning or learning. That is how Legacy Wealth is created and shared.

DAILY PRACTICE: LOOK IN THE MIRROR

Think back to the recent conflicts or negative outcomes in your life. First, remember your initial reaction and then, look closely at the situation to see where you can improve. Turn it into a Mirror Opportunity.

Reflecting on your mistakes takes courage. But once you learn to view mistakes as opportunities for growth and learning, you will find a richness in spirit you never knew was possible.

Remember that mirror work isn't about being unkind to yourself. We all make mistakes, and beating ourselves up will only undermine Principle #1, which is that we always have the power to choose a new attitude. The mistake doesn't make us a failure; it's what we do with it. I can say the same for success. Hidden in every setback is the potential for greatness if we will look for it. As Napoleon Hill once wrote, "Every adversity, every failure, every heartbreak, carries with it the seed of an equal or greater benefit."

Possessing the self-awareness necessary to acknowledge your own shortcomings is a foundational driver of growth and self-improvement. You can't change what you are unwilling to look at. Be honest with yourself, always, and see every person as a teacher who can reflect to you the areas where you need to grow. Those who are rich in spirit and wellbeing take responsibility for their mistakes and, therefore, their lives. When you practice this, building and maintaining wealth is a natural byproduct. Quit the blame game; there are no winners in it, only losers. The ability to take responsibility is a vital component of Legacy Wealth.

Are you beginning to see the pattern we have created together? As you control your attitude and express gratitude, develop your passion and take responsibility, the next Legacy Wealth Principle is sharing your values.

Chapter 5

YOUR VALUES
ARE VISIBLE

Your beliefs become your thoughts,
Your thoughts become your words,
Your words become your actions,
Your actions become your habits,
Your habits become your values,
Your values become your destiny.
—*Gandhi*

Principle: Talk is cheap. Our words have much greater meaning when backed by intentional action. Your values are what you do, not what you say. If you want to know the guiding principles behind any person's life, all you have to do is pay attention to their actions. Your values are not invisible; anyone who is watching you can tell you what they are. When our actions don't match our values, it's time for radical realignment.

A CEO of a company (whom we'll call Richard) sat in the leather armchair on the other side of my desk, red-faced and shaking. He was recounting a dishonest contract dispute that was costing him business and affecting his ability to run his own company.

"What do you want to do about it?" I asked when he finished his story and took a shaky sip of coffee.

"I want to do to him what he did to me," Richard responded without a tinge of remorse in his voice. He wanted revenge.

His response wasn't out of malice, but his hurt and anger were driving his decision. He was responding to his emotions instead of his values. This was an upstanding man, someone I've always considered honest, and someone whom I respected. I considered this for a moment and then responded, "Richard, your reputation is not for sale. Your values are not for sale. Don't let this situation compromise your integrity. Remember who you are and what you believe in."

When your emotions are running hot, it's easy to lose sight of your values. Even in tense situations like Richard's, your response, no matter how you feel, can avoid compromising your values. That doesn't mean you display weakness, but it means that you should stay in line with your beliefs. Revenge is not a demonstration of character. In fact, it's the opposite.

Legacy Wealth rests on a common set of values. As baby boomers retire, we're witnessing the greatest wealth transfer in history. Shared values within a family are critical to generational wealth transfer. Without shared values, transferring financial assets is like transferring a boat without a rudder. It will be blown off course and overturned, because the rudder isn't there to stabilize the boat. Your values are your personal and familial signposts for who you are and how you operate in life. Signposts are seen, and the bigger, brighter, and more oddly shaped they are, the more people will notice.

YOUR VALUES ARE A CHOICE

You can make a choice on how you intend to commit your lives by incorporating your values into your words, thoughts, and actions. Considering your values is the first step, but acting consistently to support your values is much more difficult. When you don't consider the signpost for your values and simply react, it creates discord and dissatisfaction. When you understand and define your core values, and then you act deliberately and with intentionality daily to support those values, you'll experience massive positive events.

The determination of your values is intensely personal. No one can determine them for you, because you must decide your own values. You have unique priorities and motivations, and the values you choose to define yourself determine your actions and level of success in your personal, family, work, and faith lives. The importance and meaning of values are for you to determine. No one can do this for you, and certainly no one can live the values through actions in place of your own decisions.

When you are deliberate about understanding your values, and use your values to guide your behavior, your impact on your family, business, and others is infinitely powerful.

HAVE A VALUES CONVERSATION

I have often thought about a conversation I had with an old friend who enjoyed substantial financial success. He was retired and had just turned 80 years old, so I decided to take him to lunch. After we ate, the conversation turned philosophical. He was in a reflective mood, so I asked him the one question I had never felt comfortable asking.

"You have accomplished so much – in your business, your impact, and your life. You seem to have conquered the mountain of success." He looked at me and nodded, waiting for my question. I asked gently, not wanting to offend him. "What is your biggest challenge right now?"

He paused for a moment, looking away as he considered his answer. "Right now, my biggest challenge is making sure that my kids don't end up as derelicts after I am gone."

My look of surprise prompted him to explain his statement. "I stay up at night, worrying that the money my kids and grandkids will inherit will deprive them of living a meaningful life."

I nodded and asked him to continue.

"I worked for everything I have, but my kids and grandkids haven't had that experience. We've tried not to give them everything, but looking back, I'm afraid that I over indulged them."

I couldn't help asking him, "What values and experience would you share with your children that you consider more important than money?"

He nodded and answered immediately. "The experience of overcoming obstacles and creating something bigger than themselves. Discovering their passion and using it in service to others. Living by a strong set of values."

I nodded and asked, "What is your values legacy–have you shared it with them?"

He laughed and shook his head. The conversation turned to other matters and the moment passed. As we were leaving the restaurant, he shook my hand in a tight grip and pulled me close to him. "Thank you for listening to an old man. You have given me much to think about."

Sharing a values conversation with your children can be the deepest way to connect with them. Instead of talking about your values, tell them stories that illustrate them. Explain why you made certain decisions in the business and the values that were behind the curtain. Ask them how they would have handled that same circumstance and what values they would use to guide them.

This isn't a one-time event. Make it a habit to look for the underlying values being followed by the people around you. Values are visible when you look for them.

VALUES ARE SEEN AND
UNIVERSALLY RECOGNIZED

The universal characteristic of a signpost is they're easily spotted. The more visible, the better. Signposts provide direction, control traffic, and lead to destinations and results. There are signposts on the road as well as in your business and family. In business, for example, the hall-mark of a great salesperson is repeated sales from the same customer. In your family, a signpost may be achievement or awards. No matter the context or situation, signposts give clarity and certainty, as well as a common framework from to guide behavior and actions.

Values signposts are no different. Our values are seen, experienced, and acted on in a way that others can see. We all know of people who, without question, we can rely on their honesty, their integrity, their hard work, their sincerity.

Like the highway signs or mileage markers, we have to be deliberate and methodical about identifying our values and priorities, and then living those values consistently. Others we interact with will notice. We evaluate others by their actions, so we therefore have to consider that the same is true, meaning that others are evaluating us by our own actions. No signpost is complete without identifying the values that are important to us, and then following that in our words and deeds.

When you are clear in your values, you will protect them from compromise, corrosion, or corruption. Knowing and operating within your values creates a set of boundaries that protect your character, your reputation, and, yes, even your finances.

WHAT YOU VALUE IS NOT FOR SALE

Before I begin a new engagement with a new business partner or client, I frequently ask the other person the following questions:

"What's important to you?"

"How can we make this relationship successful?"

"What values do you embrace in a partner?"

To start this discussion, I openly share my own values, so others understand what's important to me. Sharing values in an open discussion brings clarity to the relationships — it provides direction, clarity, and alignment. The deepest and most meaningful relationships are based on a known and common set of values.

Was there a time when you drifted from what you valued most? I've been there until I realized it was time to pay attention to how my life was speaking to me. I didn't like what my actions said about what I truly valued. It was hard to get back into alignment with who I aspired to be and who I really am. This is a process that takes a lifetime; but the most trustworthy, and therefore most successful, people are those whose values are clear in their daily actions. Make sure that who you say you are and who you really are the same. And when you wander, get clear on what matters most as soon as you can. Your Legacy Wealth depends on it.

Several years ago, a potential client tested me to determine whether I would compromise my integrity. He offered some ideas to solve a problem that were unnecessary, given the circumstances. His proposal involved a plan to destroy another person's business and professional life using damaging legal and publicity strategies. After listening to his strategy, I realized that the prospective client wanted to hurt the other person, not solve the problem. I told him that the money he would pay me for the services didn't justify making poor decisions.

Sometime later, this man told me he didn't really want to follow the destructive strategy—he was testing my values and needed to know if I would compromise my integrity when it was easy to do so, or whether my integrity would remain in place.

Many situations in life are tests. It's not a test in the sense that we can pass or fail, but a test in the sense that when we have interactions with others, they are constantly evaluating us for trust, reliability, shared interest, alignment of purpose, and simply whether they want to spend time with us. We do the same, constantly evaluate others through our involvement and interaction.

LET YOUR VALUES STAND OUT

The bigger the signpost, the more people will see it. You create your values billboards by clearly understanding your core values and demonstrably living them. Consistently, no matter the circumstances.

Like the man who is concerned about his children becoming derelicts, Legacy Wealth rests on a common set of values. We're witnessing the greatest transfer of wealth in human history, with baby boomers retiring. But what's really being transferred from one generation to the next?

When wealth is accompanied by a powerful set of values as described in this book, future generations benefit the most. Shared values within a family are critical to generational wealth transfer. Without it, the financial monies may transfer, but they will not create real Legacy Wealth.

DAILY PRACTICE: MAKE YOUR VALUES VISIBLE

Like highway signs or mileage markers, we have to be deliberate and methodical about identifying our values and priorities, and then living those values consistently. Determining your values is deeply personal, and I invite you to flip to a new page in your journal and take a moment to examine what you would consider your top 3-5 personal values. Some values you may consider in the exercise are:

Courage	*Kindness*
Dependability	*Justice*
Determination	*Learning*
Friendship	*Security*
Honesty	*Self-improvement*
Integrity	*Sincerity*

After you have identified 3-5 values that you hold dear, take a moment and rank the values in order of priority. If you can narrow the list to three pillars, all the better.

Next, inside each pillar, write a few sentences about that value and why you are committed to it. How do they relate to your purpose? If you feel stuck, here's the Legacy Wealth Values Checklist to help get your thoughts flowing:

- What character trait do I want my family to be known for?
- What values do I want my children to embody?
- What is important to me personally?
- What are my personal strengths?
- What are my core, fundamental beliefs?

- What actions by others do I feel anger?
- What actions by others do I joy?

When you are deliberate about understanding the values that create meaning in your life and live them on purpose, you can have a consistently positive impact on each person you come in contact with. When you identify your value signposts, this gives you a set of rules to act within. Instead of simply reacting to a situation, you have guidelines to determine whether your reaction is within your set of values.

As you allow your values to be seen, you'll experience massive positive events in your life. This isn't about being perfect. It is, however, about being honest. Everything you think, say, or do reflects your values; they are the meaning of your life. And everyone can see them.

Your values are visible; pay attention to your thoughts, words, and actions, and if you don't like what you notice about yourself, change it—they are a part of the legacy you're passing down to your children.

Now it's time to move on to Legacy Wealth Principle #6 – seeing every challenge as an opportunity.

Chapter 6
EVERY CHALLENGE IS AN OPPORTUNITY

"The beautiful thing about learning is that no one can take it away from you."
—B.B. King

Principle: Challenges are opportunities. Every new obstacle is a chance to grow in our own wellbeing. Adversity creates strength, and this ability to endure hard things leads to wealth. We must relearn how to learn, accepting challenges where they present themselves.

On the evening of my son's twelfth birthday, aliens abducted him. They came stealthily in the night–little green men with liquid, bulbous eyes beamed him out of his second-story window and left one of their own in his place. He looked like my son and sounded like my son, but overnight he was an altogether different boy than my smiling, obedient eleven-year-old.

My pleasant boy who cleaned his room, did his chores without complaint, excelled in school and sports, and worked well with his teachers, was gone. He wasn't abducted by aliens, but something had changed. The waves of childhood had parted for adolescence to break through. It wasn't pretty.

He was moody, uncooperative, and almost kicked out of school. During one of our many meetings with the school principal, he suggested we think about moving my son to another school and consider that he may not go to college.

When my alien son spoke to me, it was like he was a Woody doll with a string and only a few buttons that played on repeat. Instead of, "There's a snake in my boot!" I heard:

"Dad, you just don't get it," "I can't talk to you," or "You're not listening."

His grand finale always followed. "You'll never understand."

Sadly, I was one person in his life who *could* understand. I was a twelve-year-old boy once, too. However, I reacted by pushing back, disciplining more, and setting stricter boundaries. It wasn't until my wife enlightened me I realized my mistake. My son was looking for the opposite of me. He wanted more control of his life, the freedom to make his own decisions, and less interference and domination from his parents.

After my wife, Cathie, gently informed me I was being an idiot, I sat down with my son and proposed a new plan. I told him that there would still be boundaries and guardrails in his life to keep him safe from situations I believe could be harmful, but I would give him the freedom to make his own choices. If he made bad choices, he would have to accept the consequences and hold himself accountable. If he didn't take responsibility, then we would go back to locking down. He agreed.

The next twelve months were rocky as he practiced change in his life, but he eventually learned that he wanted the results more than he wanted to "be right." He learned how to make his own (good) decisions, ask for help, work as a team, and get the results in school and sports that made him proud. He also knew that being hostile and combative all the time did not get the results he wanted.

That year, my son and I were both in unfamiliar territory. Before either of us could take the next step, we had to learn how to learn in this new situation. This required humility from both of us–we had to change our initial approach to the situation and learn an entirely new one.

Today, my son is a well-adjusted, respected, and productive member of society. I'm proud of him. As Mark Twain said, "When I was a boy of 14, my father was so ignorant I could hardly stand to have the old man around. But when I turned 21, I was astonished at how much the old man had learned in seven years."

EMBRACING CHANGE

Training yourself to learn presents a beautiful opportunity for you to embrace change. Change happens regardless of whether you want it to. It is sometimes immediate, like the moment your car is rear-ended by a driver who was texting (This morning you had a bumper, and now you don't).

Change can also occur so slowly that, in my case, I didn't notice it until one day the barber held the handheld mirror up to my face, and I suddenly wondered where all the hair on the back of my head had gone.

When it comes to change, there are two kinds of people–those who view the world as glass half full, and those who cower under their beds clutching a glass half empty. Carol Dweck refers to this as the "Growth vs.

Fixed Mindset." [1] She explains that if you view your qualities as unchangeable, you'll commit your energy to proving yourself right—that you're unchangeable. This is the fixed mindset. However, if you have a growth mindset, you believe you can improve through effort.

Another way to think about it is to ask "why" versus "why not." The "why" people look at a situation, see an opportunity to try new things or learn a new skill, and will ask themselves, "Why would I do that?" Their words and thoughts jump straight to the glass half empty. They convince themselves that there is no reason to try, to learn, to grow, and therefore—don't.

The glass-half-full people ask themselves, "Why not?" when they face a new opportunity. They're eager to try something new and say yes to the opportunity, even though it may be intimidating. Instead of focusing on what could go wrong, they embrace the adventure of the challenge.

It's easy to overlook or minimize the sacrifices and challenges successful people have overcome. Wealth isn't born—it is created by wealthy people. Just like with forgiveness, learning, and growth, no one can achieve wealth

[1] Carol S. Dweck, *Mindset: The New Psychology of Success*, Ballantine Books Trade Paperback Edition, 2006.

for you. Every trial and celebration acts as a chisel that creates who you are. For example, Jeff Bezos was broke selling books from his garage. His journey to become one of the richest men in the world has many twists and turns. But his success today would not have happened unless he asked himself the question, "What is a better way to sell books?"

Most of the decisions you make are small, micro decisions, but they can add up. You can allow the past to define you and you will find yourself repeating it. Instead, learn from the past and move forward. One is extremely negative; the other is equally positive. Everything you do is a series of small decisions that culminate in larger outcomes. A long journey begins with the first step.

IDENTIFY YOUR COMFORT ZONES (THEN LEAVE THEM)

Comfort zones are only as good as our willingness to leave them. When you stay in a comfort zone for too long, that comfort zone becomes your boundaries. Those boundaries will then define you and hold you in a safe, comfortable bubble—a bubble where you aren't stretched, challenged, or presented with opportunities to sharpen your skills.

You are capable of greatness, but you may have not recognized you were at the edge of your comfort zone. To step out of your comfort zone, you must accept challenges and embrace opportunities to grow. This gives you a chance to experience life differently, with new people and in the community. If you feel bored, stuck, or unmotivated, try testing your comfort zone. And then take a bold step out of it.

Learning and stepping out of your comfort zone are the essence of self-development. As you expand your knowledge and attempt new endeavors, a constant cycle of growth and reinvention occurs. Remaining open to constant learning is the key. Use these three strategies to help you embrace new skills:

- Identify who has mastered what you want to learn;
- Find a community of people who want to learn the same thing; and
- Take action toward learning the new and becoming skilled at it.

Synergy is generated as you use these strategies to move out of your comfort zone. Let's look at each one in a bit more detail.

First, study others who have mastered the skill or

activity that you are interested in. Even though we may believe our circumstance is unique, the truth is others have likely experienced what we are going through or hope to achieve. Learn from those other people who have already gone through the pain, invested, and taken the time to learn a new skill or activity.

By nature, people are good and want to help others. I've found that people who mastered a skill or are familiar with an activity you want to try are enthusiastic about sharing their experience and wisdom. Usually, someone who has developed a skill and is good at it pursues those skills with a sense of passion. They want to talk about what motivates them, what fuels their passion. People also like to talk about themselves, what gets them excited, and to feel needed. This is especially true when you ask someone to teach you a skill or get advice that they're good at.

Second, find others who will join you. It is much easier to engage in a new activity or learn a skill when doing it with others. There's an element of accountability and shared learning when you engage with others. Think about the opportunity to attend a cooking class, learn how to play tennis, or take an MBA class. All of those activities become easier with a shared experience, with a social network to provide support.

Finally, take action. You can do all the planning and

learning you want, but you truly haven't left your comfort zone until you *do the thing* you set out to do. The more actions you take, the more confidence you build. The more confidence you build, the more you're willing to embrace new learning and change.

DAILY PRACTICE: BUILDING CONFIDENCE OVER TIME

The first time I learned to ride a bicycle, I was nervous because I was used to riding with training wheels. It happened one Saturday morning when I wandered out to the garage to get my bike. I noticed the training wheels were no longer attached and felt a bit of fear at the thought of riding without them.

Just then, my dad came outside and said, "Come on, Jim. Let's go to the driveway so you can practice."

I still remember putting my feet on the pedals and having him balance me on the bike. He gave me a gentle push to get started and told me to start pedaling. I wobbled but managed to keep enough momentum to move forward until I hit the grass. The bicycle tumbled over because I forgot to put my feet down. Unhurt and confident that I could master this skill, I jumped up and said, "Let's do it again!" It wasn't long before I was riding my bike by myself and racing with my twin sister in the alley.

That is confidence-building—one pedal push at a time.

Now take out your journal. When was the last time you left your comfort zone for something new? Write a list of the feelings and positive experiences this decision brought you.

When you're finished, start a second list. What are some things you've wanted to do, but have been too afraid to begin?

The great Rhythm and Blues singer B.B. King said, "The beautiful thing about learning is that no one can take it away from you." Once you learn to accept the obstacles of life, embrace change, and learn from all experiences, life is yours to do with as you see fit. Every challenge is an opportunity. Seeing life in this way opens you up to growth and a life rich in spirit and wellbeing, full of opportunities.

As you continue to read and learn about the Legacy Wealth Principles, remember the ground we have already covered:

- A positive attitude will carry you forward
- Gratitude is essential

- Develop your passion
- Take responsibility
- Values are visible
- Every challenge is an opportunity

I hope you can see how these Legacy Wealth Principles weave together to form a beautiful pattern. After you see and clarify the pattern, you can then share it with your children and grandchildren to ensure your legacy remains alive.

But what happens when the idea of perfection raised its ugly head? We look at it more closely in Legacy Wealth Principle #7.

Chapter 7

FAIL FAST, FIX FASTER

"You build on failure. You use it as a stepping stone. Close the door on the past. You don't try to forget the mistakes, but you don't dwell on it. You don't let it have any of your energy, or any of your time, or any of your space."
—*Johnny Cash*

Principle: Our greatest commodity is time. It's a depleting asset and our only nonrenewable resource. Once we run out, we're out—at least in this lifetime. The truly wealthy embrace failure so that they can learn whatever lessons it offers. They fail fast and fix it even faster, so that they can maintain momentum and stay on track with their goals.

As you're learning to manage your wealth—that is, your own internal system of what makes life precious—you use micro-strategies of character development. One of the most valuable of these strategies is learning how to protect your most precious, non-renewable resource: time.

A wise person uses failure to become better. To a growth-oriented person, failure is an opportunity to learn what didn't work. That's why a wise person uses failure not as a reason to quit, but as a means of success. We all fail, sometimes. We spend our precious time pursuing things that ultimately lead to a dead-end, or maybe even worse. We run head-first into our dreams, chasing our goals, and run right off the edge of a cliff. Failure can hurt; it can humiliate and frustrate the best of us. I've had more than a few encounters with this experience myself, and I can honestly say it's never been fun. That said, failure is a part of life and certainly a necessary ingredient for success. Like so many things in this book, it's what we do with our experiences that ultimately matters. With failure, the best we can do is not dwell on what didn't work, wasting even more time. Rather, we move on faster by admitting what happened, immediately addressing where we went wrong, and then trying to fix it. The faster we can do this, the better. Closing the gap between failing and fixing it is what makes a truly wealthy life.

FAIL FAST, FIX FASTER

When Thomas Edison was looking for a way to make an affordable lightbulb, he didn't quit after failing thousands of times. Instead, he said, "I have not failed. I've just found 10,000 ways that haven't worked... Every wrong attempt discarded is another step forward." In October 1879, after many attempts that looked like failure, Edison perfected the light bulb. He used what I call the Fail-Fast, Fix-Fast method. In perhaps one of Edison's most significant insights, he concluded that "Genius is one percent inspiration and ninety-nine percent perspiration." Should we focus on our failures and dwell on the past? Of course not.

The Fail-Fast Fix-Fast method means that not succeeding at something doesn't equate to failure if you use what you learned and apply it toward success. If you tried baking cookies without a recipe and on the first attempt used only one egg, your cookies would come out flat (or so my wife tells me). On the second attempt, would you follow the same recipe as the first? Of course not. You would add an egg. You keep tweaking the recipe on each attempt until you have it exactly right. In this example, a failure is simply a lesson on how *not* to bake cookies. And you can take those teachings and apply them to each subsequent batch. Genius—and might I add success—is ninety-nine percent perspiration.

You can see the impact of the Fail-Fast Fix-Fast method in the business environment. Technology and the internet were available to be used for commercial purposes, but it was the company who created a new product or service that created a new market. Called "The First Mover Advantage," For example, think of Apple, Amazon, and eBay. Each company pioneered a new way to fill a need in the marketplace.

Apple released the first iPhone in January 2007. Before that, Blackberry dominated the smartphone market, with over 50% of the smartphone sales. Nowadays, when you think of a smartphone, you probably think of a phone with a touchscreen instead of buttons. Apple did that. To have a First-Mover Advantage, the developers and leaders must take risks, focus on a specific goal and be willing to fail. Without failure, there is no success. And on the contrary, if we know what failure looks like, we can also recognize success. When you accept losses will occur, but you pivot quickly. Success will follow.

If you can't be the first in a marketplace, then you can be the next best thing—The Fast Follower. The Fast Follower sees a successful service or product, imitates their best practices, then improves on what the First Mover could have done better. Some examples are Napster versus iTunes, WordPerfect versus Word, Myspace versus Facebook, and Overture versus Google. This is the way innovation works. Change occurs one step at a time, and frequently, if not always, builds on the successes of others. When you recognize that failing fast isn't failure, but the key to success, you will always move forward.

One of a Fast-Follower's qualities is to recognize that someone else had a good idea, but that improvement is possible. In effect, instead of identifying your own "fast fail," somebody else recognizes it for you and fixes it–fast. The competitor goes to the market with a product or service that's better than yours. The ability to recognize the benefits of a competitor's strategy, but improve on that competition as a Fast Follower, is the essence of Fail Fast- Fix Fast. There's massive learning by following others who are experts in their field to examine what they do well, identify what they don't do well, and fix fast. Progress happens in the gap between using failings as a learning opportunity and implementing changes quickly to succeed. The Fast Follower recognizes the fast fix.

The same is true for each of us in our personal lives. If something isn't working, we can't do the same thing repeatedly and expect a different future result. Sound familiar? We can point to our failures as reasons we can't have future success. Continuously focusing on failings and reliving mistakes or problems that have already occurred is a waste of our greatest resource—time. We have the power to change the lens through which we view failings. We can view them as a roadmap of success.

Here's a checklist I use to stay on track with the Fail-Fast Fix-Fast method. Use the Fail-Fast-Fix-Faster Checklist to analyze a project or situation that isn't working. Ask yourself the following questions:

- What did work?
- What did not work?
- What could I have done better?
- What can I try right now as a potential solution?
- Who can I ask for their opinion on what I should do next.

THE FAST FAIL

My favorite professional sport is baseball because it's a thinking game. You might even describe baseball as the sport of the "fast fail." Great batting averages are 300, so seven out of every ten at-bats, a hitter fails. By definition, baseball players have to learn to fail fast, then take those failings and turn them into success. Any player who dwells on their failings will stay rooted in their mistakes instead of learning from them. When a pitcher is standing on the mound, the game is on his shoulders. He has about 30 seconds to erase the last pitch from his mind and focus on the next one. It's only always the next pitch that counts. The past is done. The future may be in the next pitch. The future is winning the game.

I'm the father of adult children now, and when they were growing up, I was very deliberate and methodical about guiding them to succeed. During high school, two of my kids played baseball, and the other played soccer. I would ask my kids after every game or match,

"How did it go?" Their response would be something like, "I did okay, but we still lost." Then I started asking them, "What did you learn?" A typical response would be, "I was out of position on the goal kick," or "I should've laid off that last pitch, or else I would've walked instead of striking out." When we began talking about actions that they could've taken, and they would verbalize the words that would shape their thoughts, and I could see those thoughts turn to the actions they would take to get a better result.

The progression in our discussion shifted from "How did you play?" to "What can you do to get better?" It taught my kids that they were never the victim of failure, and they always had it in them to succeed. They just had to work at it. My kids understood. They started thinking about strategies, practices, skills, and training to get better. Those thoughts would translate into positive action. I would even be so bold as to say this helped them develop critical thinking in other areas of their lives. In any situation where they see something went wrong, they have the tools to think, "How can I make it right?"

LEARN FROM THE PAST TO IMPROVE THE FUTURE

In 1981, the US military implemented a process called the After-Action Review. In a Leader's Guide to AAR's, the process is described as "a guided analysis of an organization's performance, conducted at appropriate times during and after a training event or operation with the objective of improving future performance." Learn from the past to improve the future. Designed by the US military, the AAR has four parts:

- Review what was supposed to occur.
- Establish what happened.
- Determine what was right or wrong with what happened.
- Determine how the task should be done differently next time.

The key to this review is to ensure everyone is operating from the same set of facts. Through the Fail-Fast Fix-Fast lens, make a list of all the facts that affected or shaped the events in question. When making this list, focus only on the facts—don't begin any discussion yet about a solution. Too often, people focus on how to solve a problem without reaching a consensus on the facts that led to the problem.

Try AAR in any area of your life that could be improved. There is little separation between personal matters and work when using strategies for success. Whether the discussion centers on a business project, a military operation, a child's grades at school, or a family discussion regarding money, frequently reaching consensus on the facts before any discussion of a solution will lead to a better outcome. This focus also reduces the perception that any single person is attacked or blamed. Once the facts are under control, the AAR discussion becomes much smoother and more productive.

FAILING FAST AS A LEADER

In the work-world, there are two types of managers: those who trust their employees and those who don't. The managers that trust their employees put systems in place for them to follow. They trust the employees to be accountable to these systems and get the job done. Since the employees are self-accountable, they're more likely to remain passionate about their job and take the time and effort to get it done right. The leaders align everyone with a common vision for the company, and mistakes are viewed as an opportunity to improve, thus fostering a constant mentoring environment.

The managers who don't trust their employees have an opposite outcome–they micromanage, and don't set systems in place because the manager directs even the smallest details. This type of management wears employees down. Their employees become fatigued, disenchanted, and have poorer performance.

One way you can set yourself up for success as a manager is to match specific skill sets and predispositions with the proper positions. A business leader doesn't want to put someone good at mathematics or quantitative analytics in a marketing role. We shouldn't place a person who loves to build spreadsheets and is more of an introvert in a customer-facing sales role. Recognizing these predispositions and taking action quickly helps both the employees and the company become more productive, faster. In a fast fail — fast fix environment with people, the ability to recognize whether someone is a good fit in a specific position faster always leads to better results. Simply, it's good for business.

These same principles work in your family. Every family member has a unique set of interests and skills that can be developed and enhanced. Assigning your daughter who's an artist to plan the next family vacation will probably not end well. Instead, your son who loves to build Lego sets might be better suited. Knowing the skill sets of your family and their interests can help eliminate conflict and encourage confidence.

As a leader, I've had to hire and fire many people. It's never a pleasant experience, but I've learned to see when a person's skill sets may not be suited for the job at hand. Even in the interview process, I've developed a strategy that sets accurate expectations and communicates the job description and scope of work. I cultivate an environment where employees can be honest with me and themselves if they're not successful at a job—I want to help them find the areas where they're most successful and passionate— even if it means their current position isn't working out. Sometimes an employee hasn't been suited for a position, and I helped them find a job with another company that was a much better fit for them. It's always better to recognize what is not working than to force someone to conform to a position that isn't right for them.

DAILY PRACTICE: APPLY THE FAIL-FAST FIX-FAST METHOD

You'll spend your life managing people in both your work and personal life. Applying the Fail Fast-Fix Fast method helps you recognize what interactions aren't working and fix it—fast. Try this journal exercise: Think of a perceived "failure" you've experienced recently. Now that you've learned the Fail-Fast, Fix-Fast method, what are some potential solutions to fix your problem?

The rich in spirit and well-being know not to stop at failure. They fix it (fast) instead. Be the model for your children to never give up. They're watching you more closely than you may realize.

The Fail-Fast, Fix-Fast Method works great when you want to get into action. Sometimes, though, it pays to pause. That's what Legacy Wealth Principle #8 is all about.

Chapter 8

SIT ON YOUR HANDS

"It stands to reason that anyone who learns to live well will die well. The skills are the same: being present in the moment, and humble, and brave, and keeping a sense of humor."
—*Victoria Moran*

Principle: Sometimes, the greatest action you can take is none. A two-second pause can often be the difference between a regrettable response and a wise one. Those who are truly rich know when to step back and pause to preserve a relationship. They have mastered the art of sitting on their hands.

My sister and I sat in the second row of our dad's Cherokee Six single-engine airplane. We were ten years old and loved the adventure of flying. Our mother didn't have the same enthusiasm, but she went along on these vacations, despite experiencing a lot of anxiety. As the small plane taxied down the runaway, getting faster, faster, and faster, her knuckles would turn white from gripping the armrest tightly. I could see her lips moving silently as she whispered a silent prayer.

Our dad, meanwhile, was checking the instruments, ensuring we were on course, monitoring the radio communications, the weather, and, of course, flying. Reaching cruising altitude is a process, and if you're not prepared, you could end up right where you started - on the ground.

After about twenty minutes, I felt the plane level out and the tilted suburbs below straightened back into rows of curved cul-de-sacs that gave way to fields threaded with creeks and tributaries.

Mom breathed a sigh of relief. Dad patted her on the shoulder. "We'll be in Florida in no time," he assured her. We sat in silence for the next forty minutes, admiring the vanishing cities and fortress of clouds that stretched for miles in every direction.

Then, from my right, my twin sister piped up, "I have to go to the bathroom."

Mom looked at Dad, then said, "I could use a break too." Dad took a deep breath and held it, like he did when I was four and he was about to dive to the bottom of the swimming pool to retrieve the goggles I had dropped-again. And then, he let his breath go, fiddled with the instruments, and changed course to the nearest airport so my sister (and my mom) could use the bathroom.

As an adult, two things about this instance stand out to me. First, no matter how much my dad prepared for our flight, he could only do as much as was in his power. Second, I noticed that moment my dad took a deep breath that could have ended in an explosion. Instead, he paused. That, I have learned, is the most valuable action you can take in your life: *a pause.*

A pause *is* an action. It can be two seconds or two minutes and can save you from a reaction you'll regret in the future. It was a lesson reiterated when I learned to fly.

THE ART OF SITTING ON YOUR HANDS

My dad loved flying so much that he paid for flight lessons for his sons as well. Part of the lessons for my pilot's license involved putting a hood over my eyes to only see the instruments. This trains student pilots to trust the instruments, because sometimes the visuals and perception of the world are flawed.

The first time I put the hood on and looked only at the instruments, my instructor put the plane in a steep left turn and a dive. He it so gently that I couldn't feel it. He told me to control the yolk and correct the aircraft without looking outside through the windows. The first time I did this, instead of looking at the instruments, I looked outside the window and completely panicked. I grabbed the controls, over-corrected, and made the problem much, much worse. My instructor told me to let go, and he would take over, but I was so panicked I wouldn't let go of the stick. He finally had to hit my arm to break my panic so he could take over the airplane and stabilize it.

I had forgotten the instructor's rule to "sit on my hands" when faced with a possible situation while flying. In flight training, they have conducted studies that suggest in emergency situations, the very first panicked response of a pilot-in-training was the wrong one. A panicked, untrained response usually results in an overreaction (that makes the problem worse) instead of a deliberate action.

Like flying, when faced with a problem, there are four steps to follow to "sit on your hands" instead of react. These four steps allow you to take a beat before you respond:

- Observe the facts
- Understand how you perceive and filter those facts
- Decide what strategy you will use to solve the problem
- Create a plan to take effective action

When you intentionally use these four steps, your mind stays clear and focused. Of course, you can't sit on your hands for long in an actual emergency, but you *can* do it long enough to calm yourself and get your bearings before plowing forward.

Can you think of some times in our life when you acted rashly, and the outcome wasn't what you wanted? Maybe you lashed out at your spouse in an argument, gave a curt response to a coworker, or yelled at your kids to stop fighting (always effective, right?). When yo react to a circumstance instead of pausing—however long—to act with thoughtfulness and purpose, the impact on the other person can be profound. Your quick reactions often cause pain and make the issue at hand bigger than it was initially.

THIS IS NOT PASSIVE (OR AGGRESSIVE)—IT IS POWERFUL

After I had practiced law for many years, I thought nothing would surprise me. One day, I was in a business negotiation over a merger transaction, sitting in a large conference room with a long oak table. It was a typical lawyer's office, with the hunter green pleather covered armchairs pulled up to the table and framed diplomas lining the walls. The gentleman on the other side of the transaction was getting quite animated as we discussed the transaction.

As his frustration grew, he became more animated. He stood, leaning over the table and slamming his fist onto it to punctuate each specific term he demanded. Knowing that I had to respond, but not wanting to escalate the situation, I paused for three seconds, looked at the man, then banged my hand on the table.

He leaned even further over the table toward me, glaring. "What are you doing?"

I didn't say a word. Instead, I paused a few more seconds, looked him dead in the eye, and banged my hand on the table again. Then, after a couple of seconds, I said, "I was unsure whether we were negotiating a contract or playing a game called 'Hit the table with your hand.'"

"You hitting the table won't intimidate me," he responded.

I looked at him again and repeated his statement back to him. The gentleman glanced at my client and me. He took a drink of water. "Okay. You got me. I'll calm down and let's keep negotiating." We ended up completing the deal negotiation that afternoon and closed the transaction several weeks later.

To "sit on your hands" doesn't mean to be passive. The mere act of pausing, whether for seconds, minutes, hours, or days, is itself an action. "Isn't it better to be thoughtful about the words you choose and the actions you take, especially when you're being provoked? Your response will elicit a reaction from the other person, and it's possible to choose a response that de-escalates the situation. Quick reactions to situations often end badly–think of road rage incidents, bar fights, and hate-filled words you can never take back.

I invite you to consider what I believe to be the worst part of a thoughtless overreaction. Not only are there consequences to the other person, but you must acknowledge that it could have been in your power to change the situation, not hurt someone, and maintain your self-respect.

You can't put toothpaste back in the tube. The "sit on your hands" approach always leads to a more patient, thoughtful response. Many things change for the better when you practice this. Your actions become more sustainable and consistent with your goals and desires. You cultivate a greater ability to be reliable and trustworthy. You enjoy deeper connections with like-minded people. As this practice becomes a habit, your ability to add value and positively impact other people increases over the long term.

It's ultimately empowering to know that you can, depending on the situation, pause for a second, a minute, a day before you respond and act. This strategy allows you to regain control over many situations. Realizing that a simple pause allows us to make choices more calmly and deliberately is empowering. That choice is yours and yours alone. No other person can take that choice away from you.

STRATEGIES TO HELP YOU SIT ON YOUR HANDS

I've discovered an overwhelming number of excellent strategies for "sitting on your hands." Review my short list of <u>The Top Three Ways to Remember to Pause</u>:

- Stop for a moment, breathe, and identify your emotions.

- Ask why you feel this way. Notice if you feel threatened or defensive.
- Allow your emotions to settle before responding. Focus on finding a solution.

When you can step out of the situation, even for several heartbeats, and observe yourself, it always leads to greater insight and a more thoughtful response or a more viable solution.

When someone does something or says something that causes a rise or you feel a reaction coming on, simply stop. Consider your options on how to respond and the next words you use. Maybe thinking through a response for a second or two will make all the difference in directing the discussion toward a more productive outcome. When I pause, I take a moment to identify my emotions. If I've reacted strongly to what someone said or did, I would like to understand the reason I felt that way. Processing this helps me not to take my feelings out on the other person.

We can talk about the problem until we're blue in the face, but it is the solution that brings value. Simply say out loud, "Let's work on solving the problem instead of focusing on the problem." This statement re-directs the discussion and causes everybody to consider future outcomes instead of past problems.

In recent years, I have taken to almost-daily meditation, prayer time, and yoga classes, which help calm my thoughts and actions. Directed mindfulness, breathing exercises, and physical movements designed to calm our everyday life all contribute to the basic philosophy of not overreacting to any situation. In these environments, the instructors will use words to guide the session; those words shape calming thoughts, leading to actions.

DAILY PRACTICE: REMEMBER WHEN YOU BOTCHED IT

Like virtually everything in life, the "sit on your hands" strategy takes repetition and practice to master. As you control your reactions, you regain control of your life. And like anything in life, nobody is perfect. We all need practice to get better, and part of learning a new discipline is remembering the times when it didn't go well.

Often, the best instruction is a memory of a time when we didn't take a few seconds to ground ourselves and get centered. We spoke out of turn, reacted too quickly and too strongly.

We yelled at our child, had an immature outburst ourselves, or just didn't take the time to make a good decision.

In your journal, recall a situation that you could have been handled better by sitting on your hands. What would sitting on your hands look like in that situation? What happened as a result?

And it just might be the difference between a beautiful moment and a ruined one. It never hurts to take a deep breath before you react. Learn the discipline of taking a meaningful pause. Sit on your hands. You won't regret what happens next.

The person who is wealthy in spirit knows when to act and when to pause. When you are with your family, be the calm in the storm. As you display more presence in the face of chaos, they'll notice and wonder how you are staying centered and focused. When you set the tone and energy of the situation, your children will notice and find comfort in your strength.

When you're calm and centered, a natural result is to have a servant's heart. Leadership in business and families can look quite different, but when you're a servant leader, your legacy strengthens your relationships and impact. That's what Legacy Wealth Principle #9 is all about.

Chapter 9
LEAD LIKE A SERVANT

*"If your actions inspire others to dream more, learn
more, do more and become more, you are a leader."*
—John Quincy Adams

Principle: To serve is to lead. But to lead, it is unnecessary
to serve. We must accept the mantle of leadership we all
face. To lead well, we must serve. This is the only way to
true and lasting influence. You must lead like a servant.

Our business is in the middle of a transition, as several
of my kids work there. One of my sons, who has been in
the business for several years, walked into my office and
wanted to talk. This was not unusual at all, but the look
on his face was.

"I can't be the leader in this firm as long as you are making the high-level decisions."

His statement stunned me. I thought we were working well together, and I was giving him more responsibility. Apparently, I hadn't noticed the growing signs of frustration. He had reached his limit.

While I was proud of his boldness and ambition, it was a painful moment. He no longer needed me in the day-to-day operations of the law firm. I took a deep breath and nodded at him to continue. We had a heart-to-heart conversation and walked away with a new determination to help each other.

I learned that day that I was depriving my son of the opportunity to lead and I needed to step back and serve, not direct. This was a powerful reality check for me, but absolutely correct. Sometimes the best way to lead is to let others fulfill their desire to learn, grow, and change the world. We can serve other's purpose by stepping back or stepping down and encouraging others to step up.

Anyone can be a leader. *Anyone.* If your life involves people, and every life does—then you lead. What is a leader? A leader is someone who makes decisions that impact other people. And of course, by that definition, all of us are leaders, at least at certain points in our lives.

How we make those decisions, though, dictates what kind of leader we will be.

We are leaders of many groups—our family, work, friend group, church. In a company, being a servant leader means you work to align your employees' passion with their purpose. Southwest Airlines, Tesla, Whole Foods, and The Container Store are all great examples of this. They are each well known for inspiring a higher commitment to the company through great culture, alignment of values, and servant leadership.

There are essentially two kinds of leaders: those who lead because they're in an authority position, and those who lead because they want to support and empower others to be great. Sometimes, they are the same, but not always. The person who leads by positional authority alone may achieve results from his team, but he will not have their loyalty.

A servant leader understands that those who follow have a choice to follow them. The servant leader acts on behalf of his or her followers and makes decisions for their benefit. I believe we all have an ingrained purpose to help others, and engaging in servant leadership is an essential aspect of how we both lead and serve. It doesn't matter where you were born or how you grew up. Servant leadership springs from a heart committed to helping others on their path.

THREE QUALITIES OF A SERVANT LEADER

Servant leaders have three essential qualities that are visible to their followers:

1. Identify the goals and desired outcomes you want to implement and communicate;
2. Support your people with strategies so that they can accomplish their own goals while supporting the broader company, i.e., focus on the needs of others; and
3. Lead by example and show those characteristics that foster a growth and productive environment, such as listening, self-awareness, willingness to learn, and developing trust.

First, a servant leader puts the needs of the people he leads ahead of his own. Because of this, you must understand your followers' goals and objectives and help your followers to achieve them. If you're acting out of selfishness, soon those you lead to notice and lose confidence in you. They'll eventually scatter like coins that fall through a rip in your pocket and slowly spin across the hardwood floors.

Second, a servant leader is an effective communicator. Communicate your purpose through your words, followed by actions, and people will follow. Be affirmative and supportive– never demeaning. Communicate that you care about those who follow you and have their best interests at heart. The essence of servant leadership is not dictatorial or directive, but empowering others to follow.

The third important quality of a servant leader is the ability to listen and respond to information. The combined knowledge of many is greater than the complete knowledge of one. When you listen to those you're leading, you empower them to follow and encourage them to provide ideas and solutions from a different perspective. When someone believes their voice is being heard, they're much more likely to support the project's goals and objectives enthusiastically. Listening is an art, and becoming a good listener takes practice.

When you learn to become a good listener, you'll hear what the real problem is and quickly find a solution. Servant leaders solve problems by turning them into opportunities. Their followers know they can come to the leader for help and support. As Colin Powell said, "Leadership is about solving problems. The day your soldiers stop bringing you their problems is the day you have stopped leading them. They have either lost confidence that you can help or concluded you do not care. Either case is a failure of leadership."

All of us are smarter and more capable than one of us. An organization that fosters growth, empowers people to be great, embraces new ideas and positive change, and rewards success will outperform individual effort. Servant leadership focuses on the greatness of the team. The funny thing is that you can be a servant leader in your own family.

HAVE A SERVANT'S HEART

Years ago, a friend told me, "Parents are only doing as well as their most challenging child." I reflected on that comment for a long time and realized he was right. Whenever one of my children is having a challenge, my thoughts would inevitably drift toward that child. How to help him? Is there a learning opportunity to let them fail? Do I solve the problem for them? As part of this process, I realized that my priorities inevitably centered on my kids. Important matters at work would take a back seat toward pressing personal family problems. I was a leader with my family.

Having a servant's heart is the truest way to be a servant leader. This isn't something you should pursue out of guilt, or another box you need to check off. Rather, I truly believe that we are more fulfilled when we give more than when we receive. When we give, it is with purpose and intent. We can take unconsciously. But giving? Giving is always intentional, and learning to give is a key to leading a rich, beautiful life.

Servant leadership is giving of yourself—your time and your heart—to guide others toward their greater good. Servant leadership involves aligning people's passion and purpose with the objectives of the family or business. As a servant leader, understanding the passion and motivation of the individual performers is critical to align everyone's interest with a successful result. This is true regardless of whether leadership is in personal, social, family, or business environments.

My father practiced law for fifty years. When he was in his late 80's, he still had clients. I had the privilege of being in the same legal practice for almost thirty of those years. It was toward the end of his career that I started pushing him to not accept new clients.

"Why are you taking on this client?" I asked him one day.

He looked at me and said, "Jim, I can help them in their contract negotiations." He paused and laughed. "Even though I'm an old man, I still know a thing or two."

We ended up working on the case together, and I was impressed with his clarity and strategic thinking, even at an age when most people were either dead or in a nursing home. He continued to serve others as long as he could. His passion for service impacted me, and I see continue to see his influence on my children. That is the perfect example of Legacy Wealth.

Leadership actions, however big or small, have a multiplying effect. When I placed a call to a client's office years ago, the woman who answered the phone was bright and cheery. We spoke for a few moments, and I asked her if she was this cheerful all the time. She said no, but she realized years ago that she was the first person people talked to when they were calling this company, and she wanted to do her best to brighten the mood, publicly present the company in the best light possible and help people feel good about their day. I thanked her for this attitude and jokingly asked her if I could call every Monday morning to start my week out with an uplifting and upbeat conversation. She laughed and said, "Of course, call anytime." She led every conversation, every interaction, every phone call with a message that invited engagement, optimism, and positive results. She also sets the tone for the entire organization. She was a terrific leader, showing me how to lead with a great attitude.

Anywhere there are people, you're a leader—in any situation, big or small. This can apply at work, at home, or even in line at the grocery store. Leadership isn't a button you turn on at work and turn off when you return home and recline the La-Z-Boy. Servant leadership is a value you can build in yourself and teach by example to your family members, community members, friends, coworkers, and everyone around you. It is the leadership we can all adopt today, regardless of titles.

DAILY PRACTICE:
LOOK FOR WAYS TO SERVE

Turn to a new page and write a list in your journal: What are opportunities for you to be a servant leader? How has someone been a servant leader to you? How can you serve someone better today? To lead doesn't always mean to serve. But to serve is to lead. And an important part of living a wealthy life is to lead like a servant.

When you think about your family, how have you served them? Not with money or wealth, but with yourself? If the answer is "No" or "Not really," there's no better time to start than now. Ask your family to share their idea of servant leadership and how they are using it in their life. Find out what makes them excited and passionate, and encourage them to create a meaningful life for themselves.

If you discover that either your past or the past you share with your family is a stumbling block, Legacy Wealth Principle #10 will help you. When you forgive yourself and others for the past, it opens the present and future.

Chapter 10

RELEASE THE PAST BEFORE IT CONSUMES YOU

*Forgiveness can make us a better person but does it
make a better leader? An eye for an eye for an eye
for an eye…ends in making everyone blind.*
—Mahatma Ghandi

Principle: What's done is done. Clinging to the past destroys opportunity and wastes our most valuable resource, time. Releasing the past before it consumes us is the only sensible plan of action. Otherwise, our old hurts and pain impact every decision we make in our personal and professional lives.

"The past is prologue," as Shakespeare says, and this is true, but I'd like to add to his quote. How we *feel* about the past is prologue. Whether we release it or cling to it like Saran Wrap on a Bundt pan, the difference is that the past can't save you. The past can captivate you, ensnare you, and control your future, if you let it. The past is prologue. Yes, we know that. But let me back up. Over the years, I've learned that how I react to past situations—whether I forgive or never let go—affects the bounty I enjoy in my present and future lives. Forgiveness is liberating, and when we learn to let go of what was, we become kinder, more joyful people. We learn to enjoy what is.

Years ago, I was exiting a business relationship with someone I had become relatively close to. I'd shared the usual confidences you share with close friends–my hopes and dreams, and even my fears for my brother, who has a severe mental and physical disability. When we had a disagreement during our exit plan, he crafted the confidences I entrusted him with into a knife, then twisted it into my back. Afterward, I played his angry words on repeat—they were a shadow standing over me as I shaved my face, when I drove home from work, and even when I spent time with my family. I sat in the anger, hurt, and betrayal. I let his words and my unforgiveness control me.

Finally, one day I decided enough was enough. That friendship hadn't gone the way I had hoped, and I let myself feel sadness, hurt, and anger. And then I moved on, because I wasn't going to let him continue to hurt me and my family through the memory of his angry words. Forgiveness releases the past so that we can move forward.

FORGIVENESS LEADS TO CLEAR COMMUNICATION

Forgiveness, much like staying healthy, isn't something anyone else can do for you. It's not contingent on apology or contrition from someone you feel wronged you—you have to forgive yourself first. Forgiveness is an ongoing process of self-leadership.

It doesn't matter if the conflict or hurt happened in a personal or business context, forgiveness of yourself is always the first step. Your perception of the other person's behavior may be clouded by your past, unresolved wounds. Their behavior may also be clouded by their past. In one sense, when two people have unresolved and unforgiven issues, it is their past that becomes entangled in conflict. It's almost as if each person's past is informing their present behavior. There is no clear communication, because the energy, words, and actions of each person is clouded by the past.

Forgiveness clears the path toward the ultimate objective of Legacy Wealth, which is to share the values and beliefs that created the financial, mental, physical, emotional, and spiritual wealth of the family. When there is discord and conflict between two people or inside a business, the dynamics of the past impinge on the current situation. When forgiveness has cleansed the past, everyone feels respected and honored. But how do you handle an adverse situation that impedes the goal?

One year, I was involved in the sale of a company that was part of a legacy plan, a family succession. The sale was difficult, because the professionals on the other side of the negotiation enjoyed conflict and constantly tried to bait, create chaos, object and create frustration in order to wear down opposition and get their desired result. Every email, every phone call, and every touchpoint was designed to be oppositional. I had to use an arsenal of tools, including learning from every touchpoint, adopting communications going forward, not getting distracted by meaningless words, staying focused on the purpose and objective, and showing that we were determined to get the right result. I also used forgiveness as a tool to avoid reacting to the other side's difficult messaging.

The challenge throughout the process was to provide clear and active communication, demonstrate our position and objective, but not create such a high level of conflict that communication would break down. In short, we responded with kind assertions to every nasty email, assuring the company that we intended to see the deal through. Once we made this clear, they changed their tune, and we completed the succession.

The past does not equal the future, and you can win over others who aren't playing nice. When you know your objectives and clearly see your goals, forgiveness is like a secret weapon. The other side will not understand why you aren't taking their bait, and eventually, they will concede.

HOW LONG HAVE YOU BEEN HOLDING IT?

A teacher walks into class with a pitcher of water. At the front of the classroom, she holds the pitcher in her hand and asks her students, "How much does this pitcher weigh?"

As the students call out answers, she entertains a few of them. Then she asks another question: "Doesn't it depend upon how long you hold the pitcher?"

What a great analogy! The longer you hold the pitcher, the heavier it becomes. The weight of water hasn't changed, but your ability to hold the pitcher up changes, and it feels heavier as time passes. If we choose to hold on to problems longer, relive upsetting events in our minds, and talk about negative occurrences over and over, the issues seem to get worse. The longer we focus on past problems, dwell on them, talk about them, and act on them, the heavier the pitcher becomes.

There is no "delete" button for past events. The question becomes how you are perceiving the past and at what cost. In business and personal relationships, there is always another way to see the conflict. When you can put yourself in the shoes of the other person and consider their viewpoint, it opens a window to forgive. Empathy for the other person's struggles is one aspect of forgiveness that leads to healed relationships.

Another aspect is your degree of emotional control. When you feel anger rising in your body, that is the time to "sit on your hands" and take a deep breath. Intentional breathing calms the nervous system and the "flight or fight" reaction. Turn away from the trigger to give yourself time to step out of the anger. As your energy shifts from anger to neutral, your response will also change and deescalate the situation.

Holding the pitcher of anger, hurt, resentment, or betrayal can lead to unintended consequences. Numerous studies have shown that bitterness and hatred create stress, depression, and disease. The benefits of forgiveness and letting go improve well-being, lower blood pressure, and increase longevity.

LETTING GO TO DISCOVER THE LESSON

Legacy Wealth comes from acting with purpose and having an acute sense of self to maintain emotional and psychological control of yourself. Despite what life throws at you, your choice to forgive the past so you can create intentionally in the present is a signpost of Legacy Wealth. When your past doesn't pollute the present, you are free to create a lasting impact on those around you.

A close friend of mine was diagnosed with pancreatic cancer, which has a 95% fatality rate. But the impossible happened—he survived. One day at lunch, he tearfully shared that he was grateful for the diagnosis. My surprise was obvious and he laughed.

"Jim, I know it sounds crazy, but being diagnosed with cancer was the shock I needed. It made me take stock of my life and priorities. Instead of 70-hour weeks, I spend time with my family. I've re-engaged in my church and renewed old friendships. I know it sounds like a cliché, but each day is truly a miracle."

"How did you reach this place of acceptance?" I couldn't help asking.

He grew thoughtful for a moment, thinking back over his journey. He finally looked up at me and said, "I had to forgive myself, my past, and especially God."

I nodded and asked, "Are you glad you went through this experience?"

"Absolutely! I was so focused on pilling up wealth that I forgot to nourish my true wealth, the relationships I have with my family, friends, and of course, God."

Like my friend, you may have experienced just as devastating a diagnosis or event. Hopefully, you also experienced the power of forgiveness and the door it opens to learning more about yourself and your relationships. Life is a series of learning experiences that foster growth and maturity.

If you spend your time in bitter regret, harboring and keeping anger and resentment and hostility for those who may have wronged you, then your past defines your future. Choosing to see the present through the lens of the past is always tempting, but never constructive unless you have forgiven. Accepting the past, letting go of resentment or anger, and accepting circumstances as a learning opportunity puts you in the best position to spend your most important commodity, your time.

To remind you to use forgiveness as a necessary tool, I created the Legacy Wealth Forgiveness Steps. When you feel triggered by an external event of person, take a deep breath in and hold it for four seconds. Release it slowly and ask the following questions:

- Why am I doing this?
- Respond with kindness to everyone, regardless of their attitude or how you feel.

Visualize the outcome you want before you take respond or take action.

Learning this process, notice that you will begin to see the lessons hidden inside the problem. Instead of wasting time reacting from a trigger, you can respond more effectively. Repeating this approach over and over creates synergy and uses time wisely.

Make no mistake-time is a currency just like money. You can save it, hoard it, spend it, and use it in ways that accomplish your goals and move forward. Both you and your legacy are defined by how you spend your time.

DAILY PRACTICE: RELEASE PAST HURTS

Take out your journal. Write a list of instances in the past that you need to release. For each item on your list, take a moment to consider what you need to do to let the past go. Only when you face the past can you truly release old wounds from the control, they wield over you. Look at the past hurts you've experienced and caused and let them both go. All of them. Don't dwell on guilt or shame; stare your greatest sins in the face and choose to forgive yourself, as well as anyone who has wronged you. The only way we can have a brighter future is by letting go of the past and releasing its control over us.

Conclusion:
A Truly Wealthy Life

A long journey begins with the first step. So let me say: Congratulations, you've just finished the first step of an incredible journey. Empowering yourself to design and create a passion-filled life that you share with others is the ultimate form of wealth. If there is one lesson I've learned, it is that we can take control of our actions, our perspective, and how we use our time. We can and should follow our passions our entire lives to the end. Creating wealth can make us rich and have lots of money. Creating Legacy Wealth also empowers your life and impacts the lives of those around you. There are people who are rich in money but are stingy and uncaring. In contrast, there are others who are not wealthy in their bank accounts, but are wealthy in life because they are generous, grateful, and giving.

The eye-opening realization is that you get to choose. You have control over yourself and your wealth. Your legacy is shaped by how you define wealth. Hopefully by now, your definition has expanded to include all aspects of wealth.

If you want to build a wealthy life, remember that money doesn't make you rich. What makes you rich is Legacy Wealth—well-being in every area of your life. When you consider that your choice to incorporate and embed the Legacy Wealth Principles in your life has long-lasting consequences, the quote that opened this book gains deeper meaning. Allow me to repeat the quote and consider how it applies to you and your family.

Blessed are those who plant trees under whose shade they will never sit.

You have planted the seeds and tended the roots of the tree to produce a magnificent harvest. You have read this book because you are concerned about the future generation. There is still time to use the Legacy Wealth Principles to ensure your wealth tree produces shade for your children's children.

A wealthy life is created with intention, purpose, and practice. It doesn't have to be difficult or complicated. Practice daily and get better at dealing with the challenges and opportunities that life presents. A simple life with no significant accomplishments isn't a life well lived. When you accept every aspect of your life, including the experiences you didn't ask for, you grow stronger. Strength empowers perspective and purpose. Saying yes to what life brings you, being grateful for it all, and choosing to move forward with what you have is the making of a rich life.

As the greatest transfer of wealth continues, make sure that you also transfer the positive attitudes, gratitude, passions, values, opportunities, failures, presence, service, and forgiveness that molded your life's work. Remember, your Legacy Wealth lives on in those who follow you.

Leave your greatest legacy with your children. Start now and define what "wealth" means to you and begin sharing it with those you love. Remember, money is accumulated, wealth is created. Lasting wealth transcends money and shapes generations to come.

About the Author

Jim Shields is a serial entrepreneur, strategic investor, and successful attorney with over three decades of experience. His experience is primarily in supporting founder-led businesses, managing complex commercial business litigation, and representing financial institutions. He is currently the CEO of <u>The Shields Group</u> and founder of <u>Shields Legal</u>.

At The Shields Group, Jim and his operating team partners with private companies to grow and complete successful transactions. Jim also helps company founders transition after the sale and preserve their family legacy. Shields Legal is a full-service law firm that specializes in commercial transactions, business litigations, and grooming businesses for a prospective sale. The systematic, proprietary process used by the attorneys is called <u>Growth to Exit©</u> and it prepares your business for prospective buyers.

Jim grew up in the Dallas area and attended Jesuit College Prep High School and Saint Mary's University for his undergraduate degree and law school. Besides his legal and business successes, in 2013, Jim launched a community involvement project called IMPACT 365, which inspires each individual in his firm to take intentional action every day to help someone. Supporting his community and fostering the talents of young entrepreneurs are strong passions. He is also heavily involved in the Communities Foundation of Texas for Business, which supports charities in North Texas and helps small businesses give back. He and his wife, Catherine, share three adult children who are all successful in their own right and involved in the business.

Additional Resources

Is your privately owned company ready to sell?
Do you know what buyers or investors
look for when they value a company?
How do you increase your company's value
before a potential buyer considers it?

Shields Legal is a law firm with deep experience representing sellers of privately owned businesses. We focus on the five key areas of your company that are most likely to add or subtract value, and we help you embed best practices in each area.

- Legal (contract review, corporate governance, risk management)
- Finance/Accounting (review of capital and debt structure, A/R needs, growth capital needs, audits, ICFR)
- Human Capital (policies/procedures, compensation aligned with roles, compliance)
- Sales/Marketing (sales process, compensation, marketing & messaging alignment)
- IT/IP systems (operating software, data security, disaster recovery plan)

You want to preserve and protect your
life's work. We help you do that.
Please reach out to <u>Shields Legal</u> to learn more.

A Note of Gratitude

My heartfelt thanks go out to you for buying, reading, and sharing this book. I have personally witnessed too many families torn apart by focusing on the money instead of sharing the transfer of values, such as the Legacy Wealth Principles.

My passion is to connect with as many people as possible to share the importance of preserving the wealth legacy, as well as the financial and asset transfer. My goal is to provide a different outlook on the topic of wealth transfer to ensure that the principles that created the wealth are seen, recognized, and adopted by the next generation.

Now that I am a grandfather, I see many of these principles being taught to my grandchildren. There is nothing more deeply satisfying than to see your children raising the next generation to become well-rounded, productive, and servant leaders.

I do have a favor to ask. Would you please take a moment and leave me a five-star review on Amazon? Your comments about the takeaways are also appreciated.

Thank you for spending your time with me.

- Jim Shields

Made in the USA
Columbia, SC
16 November 2024